People to Know Today

Bill Gates
Computer Mogul and Philanthropist

Michael A. Schuman

Enslow Publishers, Inc.
40 Industrial Road
Box 398
Berkeley Heights, NJ 07922
USA

http://www.enslow.com

Library of Congress Cataloging-in-Publication Data

Schuman, Michael.
    Bill Gates : computer mogul and philanthropist / Michael A. Schuman.
        p. cm. — (People to know today)
    Includes bibliographical references and index.
    ISBN-13: 978-0-7660-2693-3
    ISBN-10: 0-7660-2693-0
    1. Gates, Bill, 1955–   2. Businesspeople—United States—Biography—Juvenile literature.
3. Computer software industry—United States—History—Juvenile literature. I. Title.
    HD9696.C62G3367 2007
    338.7'610053092—dc22
    [B]   2006038482

Printed in the United States of America

10 9 8 7 6 5 4 3 2 1

To Our Readers: We have done our best to make sure all Internet addresses in this book were active and appropriate when we went to press. However, the author and publisher have no control over and assume no liability for the material available on those Internet sites or on other Web sites they may link to. Any comments or suggestions can be sent by e-mail to comments@enslow.com or to the address on the back cover.

Illustration Credits: Alan Berner/ Seattle Times, p. 14; AP/Wide World Photos, pp. 17, 20, 31, 39, 55, 57, 59, 75, 77, 80, 93, 97, 99, 103; Barry Wong/ Seattle Times, p. 9; Corbis Corporation, p. 47, 84; Getty Images, pp. 24, 61, 89; Microsoft Corporation, pp. 1, 4, 64, 69; Time Life Pictures/ Getty Images, pp. 43, 107.

Cover Illustration: Microsoft Corporation.

CONTENTS

Bill Gates

CELEBRATING WITH A SHIRLEY TEMPLE AND ICE CREAM

Who would have thought that a simple magazine article would be responsible for changing the way billions of people live?

Harvard University sophomore Bill Gates and his friend Paul Allen found themselves fascinated by an article in the January 1975 issue of *Popular Electronics*. The subject was a new invention: a very primitive computing machine called the Altair. It had been designed by an Air Force veteran, Henry Edward (Ed) Roberts and his friend, Bill Yates. Roberts and Yates were running a computer business called Micro Instrumentation and Telemetry Systems, Inc., or MITS, in the high desert city of Albuquerque, New Mexico.

Gates and Allen were nineteen and twenty-one years old respectively. They had been toying with

A Modern Marvel Almost Four Centuries in the Making

Though many people view the computer as a fairly recent invention, the ideas that led to its development span more than three hundred years. The seventeenth-century French mathematician, physicist, and philosopher Blaise Pascal invented the first automatic calculator in 1642. In the 1820s, Charles Babbage, an English mathematician, developed the idea for a programmable computer—which he called an "analytical engine"—but he lacked the funds to actually build it. In 1888, Herman Hollerith, an American statistician, invented a machine that used a punch card system to tabulate the results of the 1890 census. He founded the Tabulating Machine Company, which became the Computing-Tabulating-Recording Company (C-T-R) in 1911, and finally the International Business Machines Corporation (IBM) in 1924.

World War II saw a number of technological advancements. Harvard University professor Howard Aiken constructed a digital computer called the Mark 1, which operated through the use of relays, or switches. A year later, John Presper Eckert, Jr., and John William Mauchly, engineers at the University of Pennsylvania, built the ENIAC (Electronic Numerical Integrator And Computer), one of the earliest general-purpose computers. Over the next seven years, the ENIAC evolved into the UNIVAC, the first commercially successful computer. The 1960s saw the creation of the integrated circuit, or microchip, which allowed engineers to develop microcomputers and fast and powerful main-frames. In 1971, Intel's microprocessor chip further downsized the computer to the personal level most people are familiar with today.

computers for years and had even earned money working with them back in their hometown of Seattle, Washington. In 1975 they were a long way from home. Harvard is in Cambridge, Massachusetts, roughly three thousand miles from Seattle. Allen was working at a computer company called Honeywell, in Boston, Massachusetts. Boston is just across the Charles River from Cambridge.

Computers had been around for more than thirty years, but had been used mainly by the military and large businesses. They were massive machines, known as mainframe computers. At first they were so huge that a single computer occupied an entire room. Gradually they got smaller, but the smallest at that time was still about the size of a refrigerator.

After Gates and Allen read about the Altair, they thought this may be the start of the next trend in computers: a microcomputer, or small, personal computer any person could use.

Computers, known as hardware, need programs, or software, to make them work. Gates and Allen read in the article that the only software that would work with the Altair was an 8080 machine language. It was a very complicated language that a nontechnical person could not use easily. The two young men felt they could design a program for the Altair that even those who got D's in math could use with little trouble. That was despite the fact that many computer experts said it could not be done.

Gates and Allen placed a long-distance call to Ed Roberts. They told Roberts that they had developed a computer program that would work easily with the Altair. It was in a computer language called Beginner's All-Purpose Symbolic Instruction Code, known by its acronym, BASIC. BASIC users communicated with the computer by using two characters. In most cases, these were the numbers one and zero.

There was one problem, however. Gates and Allen had not yet developed such a program. Ed Roberts was no fool. Several people had called him after the article about the Altair appeared. They all told Roberts they could design an easy-to-use program for his computer. Roberts answered them all by saying that he would believe it when he saw it.

Gates and Allen worked day and night most of that winter. They turned to another Harvard student named Monte Davidoff for additional technical advice.

As for Gates, he was so driven that he skipped classes to work on the program. It seemed like Allen and he spent all their time in the university's Aiken Computer Lab. They tried getting by on an hour or two of sleep a night. Sometimes they would take quick naps in the computer lab. Other times, Gates's body simply wore out and he fell asleep sitting at a lab desk.

After eight weeks of almost nonstop work, Gates

Paul Allen and Bill Gates (left to right) discuss product strategies in 1982.

and Allen were ready. Plans were made for Allen to fly to Albuquerque to make the presentation to Roberts. Gates would stay at Harvard.

As confident as Gates was, he had last minute jitters. If there was even a minor mistake in the operating system, their software system would fail. The night before Allen was to leave, Gates warned, "Paul, if I've got one of these opcodes [operating codes] wrong, this thing is just not gonna work."[1]

Allen decided to get a good night's sleep to be prepared for his presentation the next day. Meanwhile, Gates stayed up all night going over every program detail. The next morning, he wished his friend well as Allen boarded his flight to Albuquerque.

Allen arrived in Albuquerque and was disappointed to see that Roberts's company, MITS, was a small outfit located in an office in a rundown part of the city. He had expected a prosperous and professional business.[2] MITS was hardly a top-of-the-line computer company like Honeywell.

Allen spent that night in Albuquerque in a hotel. He called Gates back in Cambridge, telling him how disappointed he was when he saw the MITS office. Both Gates and Allen were worried that MITS was a joke and that they had wasted two months of time and effort.[3]

But Allen was already in Albuquerque, so it made no sense to call it quits now. The next morning, Roberts drove Allen from the hotel to his office. The time had come to test Gates's and Allen's BASIC program, which was on a paper tape.

Allen started feeding the paper tape into the Altair. Roberts and Yates looked on. As Allen continued feeding the paper tape, Roberts and Yates laughed quietly, thinking there was little chance a software program designed by a nineteen-year-old college student and his twenty-one-year-old friend would work.[4]

After loading the tape for fifteen minutes, Allen, Roberts, and Yates waited.

They did not have to wait long.

The Altair responded. The teletype connected to the Altair printed out the words: "memory size?"

Allen answered the computer, typing in more instructions. The computer obeyed.

The personal computer industry was born right there, in a ramshackle storefront in New Mexico. Roberts was ready to make a deal with Gates and Allen.

After Allen flew back to Boston, he and Gates toasted their good fortune. Since Gates was too young to drink alcohol legally, he celebrated the beginning of this new frontier with a dish of ice cream and a nonalcoholic drink called a Shirley Temple.

2

LAKESIDE MOTHERS CLUB TO THE RESCUE

Bill Gates was born on October 28, 1955, in Seattle, Washington. His real name is William Henry Gates III. The Roman numeral III indicates that he is the third male in his family with that name. His grandfather and father were also named William Henry Gates. Because he was the third William Henry Gates, he was given the nickname Trey by his family members. When he was not called Trey, he was known by his family as Little Bill.

Bill Gates grew up in a well-to-do home. His father was an attorney who worked for one of Seattle's most highly respected law firms. His mother, Mary Maxwell Gates, became a schoolteacher after graduating college.

Mary's first child was a girl named Kristianne, born in 1953. After the birth of her daughter, Mary gave up teaching to stay at home and raise her family. When she had spare time she did volunteer work. One of the groups she volunteered for was the local Museum of History and Development.

Part of her museum duties included going to local schools to speak about Seattle's history. Teaching was in her blood, and she enjoyed bringing artifacts from the museum to show kids in their classrooms. At the time, Bill was too young to attend school, so Mary often took him with her on her volunteer missions. He would sit on the teacher's desk as his mother showed relics of Seattle's history to older kids.

Bill was a skinny child with a head of blond hair combed backward. He also had a ton of energy. One of his favorite toys was a rocking horse. He would literally spend hours rocking back and forth on the toy horse. He seemed to get lost in thought while on it. His mother, Mary, said, "I think that got to be a very comforting, comfortable kind of motion for him."[1]

When he started public school, Bill was the youngest child in his class. The Seattle public-school system's cutoff date for deciding a student's grade level was November 1. Since Bill's birthday was October 28, he just made the cut for the higher grade. As a result, he was not only the youngest, but he was almost always the smallest and most awkward kid in class.

However, he was also one of the smartest. One pleasure trip that impressed him most as a child was

Bill's mother, Mary Gates (above), served on the boards of United Way, First Bancorp, and many other corporations. She died in 1994.

not to an amusement park or the beach. It was his visit to an exposition called the Seattle World's Fair. It took place in 1962, when Bill was just six years old.

In the days before theme parks became common vacation destinations, people visited world's fairs. World's fairs showcased the latest advancements in technology along with the cultures from different countries. Most also contained a midway, filled with rides and games. World's fairs still take place, but they are not the major events as they once were.

World's fairs occur in different cities across the world every few years, and vacationers often travel thousands of miles to see them. Luckily for Bill, the 1962 world's fair was in his hometown.

The theme of the 1962 world's fair was Century 21. Its symbol was a tall tower called the Space Needle, which had a revolving restaurant at the top. The pavilions at the fair displayed technology that experts predicted would be common in the year 2000.

Time has shown many predictions were off base. One was that "supersonic air travel will allow people to circumnavigate the world in minutes."[2] Another was that people will wear rocket belts "that enable a man to stride thirty feet."[3]

On the other hand, several predictions turned out to be true. One was that "men living today will land on the moon."[4] Although hard to believe in 1962, that event took place just seven years later. Another prediction was that there would be both push-button and cordless telephones. Of course, those are in common use today.

One other prediction was that "home computers will be used for 'record-keeping, shopping and check-writing.'"[5] Like traveling the world in just minutes, this prediction seemed like science fiction. Computers were in their infancy in 1962.

Like most six-year-old children who visited the 1962 Seattle World's Fair, Bill loved hopping on board the mile-long monorail and experiencing some of the other fast-paced rides. Unlike many children that age, he also liked the technical exhibits. He said that he and his family went to every pavilion.

The world's fair aside, most of Bill's days were spent at View Ridge Elementary School. Outside of school, he liked playing board games with his family and card games with his grandmother, Adelle Maxwell. His grandmother, known as Gam, loved cards and taught Bill to play children's games, such as go fish. By spending time with his grandmother, he also learned how to play bridge.

When she was a young girl, Gam had been both a scholar and a starting forward on her high-school women's basketball team. She was also her high school's valedictorian, the student with the best grades of the entire class. To Gam, card games were not merely fun and recreation. They were a means to use one's brains and ability to strategize.

Although Bill Gates was from a privileged home, his parents tried to make sure he was not spoiled. He was allowed to watch television only on weekends. He was encouraged to spend spare time on weekdays reading, and he loved doing so. In fact, when he was eight, he set a lofty goal for himself—to read the entire *World Book Encyclopedia* straight through. He made it as far as the letter "P," when an updated edition was released. Instead of tackling a whole new edition, he decided to stop at that point.

In school, Bill liked science and math best. The gawky, towheaded boy could add and multiply more quickly and accurately than most of his classmates. He was good at organizational skills. Because of that, he was given a special job by the school librarian. When books were missing, Gates was assigned to track them down. Sometimes, he worked through recess to find the missing books. His teachers would force him to

leave the library to go outdoors and relax and play.

Since they wanted Bill to have social skills as well as good grades, his parents suggested that he join a local Scout troop. So he became a member of Cub Scout Pack 144. He had fun taking part in the Cub Scouts' activities. When Bill was old enough, he joined Boy Scout Troop 186. Because of his scouting activities, he learned to enjoy the outdoors as well as the classroom.

William Gates, Sr., and his second wife, Mimi, oversee the administration of vaccines against diptheria, tetanus, whooping cough, and hepatitis B in Mozambique, Africa, in 2001. Gates Sr. always encouraged the charitable efforts of his son, Bill.

Most of the activities consisted of day hikes in the mountains around Seattle. He often showed his fellow Scouts that he could be a fun guy outdoors as well as a math whiz in the classroom. A day hiking trip on Vancouver Island, across the Washington state border in Canada, involved crossing a suspension bridge. Bill decided to put some excitement into the trip. Troop 186's newsletter covered the adventure by saying: "This return was 'livened' when Bill Gates decided to jump up and down on the suspension bridge, creating the enormous mirth which you can imagine among the others on the bridge."[6]

On another occasion, his troop embarked on a week-long, fifty-mile hike. Bill wore a new pair of boots that were not suitable for such a long trek. After only two days, his feet were sore, blistered, and bleeding. Yet he wanted to continue. By the time the troop had marched twenty-five miles, Bill could barely stand. He had no choice but to leave the trip. His mother was called to take him home.

When Bill was in fourth grade, his parents moved the family to a rambling new home three miles away in a wealthy town called Laurelhurst. Bill also attended a new school, Laurelhurst Elementary. That same year, Mary gave birth to her third child, a girl they named Libby.

It was also about this time that Bill began having trouble in school. He continued to get A's in the subjects he liked, such as the sciences, math, and reading. In the subjects he did not care much about, such as penmanship, he got C's and D's. His older sister, Kristi, was constantly receiving straight A's. Bill's parents made a deal with their son. If he got straight A's he would be allowed to watch television on weeknights. It did not work. Bill had become bored with much of what his public school had to offer.

In sixth grade, Bill's teachers suggested that he take part in an extracurricular activity known as the Contemporary Club. The kids who joined were some of the school's brightest. They would get together and discuss the day's current events or books they had recently read. Other times, they would play games that called for intelligence and strategy. A classmate named Stanley Youngs said that Bill's favorite game was Risk, in which the object is taking over the world.

In spite of his intelligence, as Bill got older he started showing behavioral problems in school. He would goof off in class, sometimes breaking up laughing as the teacher was talking. His school desk was always a complete mess. At home, his room was also a constant pigsty. His mother begged him to pick up his clothes and straighten out his room. But just as his parents could not get Bill to earn straight A's, they also could not get him to clean his room. Finally, his parents told their son to just keep his bedroom door shut so no one would have to see his room.

The Gates family spent their summers at a water-front camp called Cheerio. Some of the Seattle area's richest families spent their summers there. Bill learned

Bill Gates answers audience questions during the third annual TechNet Innovation Summit at Stanford University in November 2006. Gates's interest in computers took root when he was in the seventh grade.

to water ski at Cheerio. A Gates family friend named Brock Adams taught Bill to play tennis, and he became a very skilled tennis player. It was Adams who had introduced Mary and Bill, Jr., to each other many years earlier. The families often competed with their own version of camp Olympics with events such as capture the flag, egg toss, and relay races.

Still, Bill's parents were concerned about his school problems. They thought he was immature and needed discipline. So for the seventh grade, in 1967, they sent him to private Lakeside School. Lakeside was an all-boys prep school, and Bill did not like the idea of going there.

He said, ". . . when I was in 6th grade, and my mom and dad suggested I go to Lakeside, I wasn't too sure about it. In those days, Lakeside was an all-boys school where you wore a jacket and tie, called your teachers 'master,' and went to chapel every morning. For a while, I even thought about failing the entrance exam."[7]

He did go to Lakeside, but had trouble adjusting. His new classmates were the sons of the wealthiest and most powerful families in the Seattle region. Instead of receiving all A's in his favorite subjects as he usually did, Bill was nearly a straight B student.

In time, he became acquainted with several boys who became his friends. By the end of seventh grade, in mid-1968, he also became closely acquainted with something else: the computer.

It was just six years since Bill had first encountered the science of computers at the Seattle World's Fair. In that short period of six years, big advancements had been made. Computers no longer needed to occupy the entire wall of a room to be functional. A company named Digital Equipment Corporation (DEC) was now selling a minicomputer. It was about the size of a refrigerator, but by early 1960's standards, it was miniature.

Technology was on the minds of many of America's educators. Just ten years earlier, the Soviet Union won the first leg of the space race when they became the first nation to send a human into outer space. Americans were humiliated. As a result, they demanded that science education should be a priority in schools. In 1968, humans had not landed a man on the moon, but the U.S. National Aeronautics and Space Administration (NASA) was preparing for that. Computers were an integral part of the space program.

The Lakeside staff decided it was important to make an investment in technology. They would introduce their students to the new universe of computers.

But how would they do so? Computers were very costly, and even a private school as wealthy as Lakeside could not afford to buy one. Instead, they decided to buy a teletype machine. It was installed in a campus building called McAllister Hall. Students used the teletype by typing a command on the machine. The command would be sent through a telephone wire to a Program Data Processor (PDP-10) minicomputer in downtown Seattle.

Computer time was not free. The PDP-10 was owned by a famous corporation, General Electric (GE). GE billed Lakeside school for the computer time used by its students. A volunteer group at the school, the Lakeside Mothers Club, decided to pay for computer usage by holding a rummage sale, where secondhand objects are sold. They raised three thousand dollars and thought it would last the rest of the spring until the school year was finished.[8]

However, the three thousand dollars was gone within a matter of weeks. The boys who excelled in math and science took to the new device eagerly. Most were upperclassmen, but one was the sandy-haired, skinny, seventh-grader Bill Gates. He had to fight with older kids for computer time. When he was able to get time, Bill took full advantage of it. The first computer program he ever designed was a tic-tac-toe game, using the computer language BASIC. He then designed a moon-landing game, and in time, taught the computer to play Monopoly.™

Gates had several friends who enjoyed toying around with him on the computer system. One was Kent Evans, also a seventh grader. Another seventh

Photos taken in the early 1970s of Microsoft's founding partners, Bill Gates (left, top and bottom) and Paul Allen (right) are shown on display here at the Microsoft Visitor Center in Redmond, Washington, in April 2005.

grader was a tall, skinny boy named Richard Weiland. A third was a pudgy ninth grader named Paul Allen. Although Allen was two years older than Gates, he often went to Bill for help with computer problems. Gates and Allen became friends and visited each other's homes. Gates was most astounded by Allen's huge collection of science-fiction books.

This would be the beginning of a lifelong friendship and the start of something big.

3

BUGS IN THE MACHINES

Bill Gates, Paul Allen, and the other boys in their group seemed to spend every spare minute in the computer room. Because computers had been used mainly by the military and businesses, teachers as well as students were learning together about these magical machines. For example, on one occasion, one teacher used up two hundred hours of costly computer time by accidentally running an infinite loop, or a set of instructions that the computer continuously follows without end.

The teacher in charge of the computer room was Fred Wright. Bill Gates said, "Fred Wright really inspired me to learn math, and [he] was a great mentor in the computer room in McAllister Hall."[1]

Although Bill Gates was mesmerized by computers,

his interests extended beyond the ways machines worked. If Paul Allen was not reading science-fiction books, he was often busy poring over the pages of a magazine such as *Popular Mechanics*. While Bill wanted to learn some of the fun things computers were capable of doing, he was also interested in ways he could use the computer to earn money. So when he was in eighth grade, he started his first business. It was

> **When he was in eighth grade, he started his first business . . . the Lakeside Programmers Group.**

called the Lakeside Programmers Group. Aside from Bill Gates, the group consisted of his friends Paul Allen, Richard Weiland, and Kent Evans.

Their first job almost fell into their laps. The group did not make money from it, but they got something almost as valuable: free computer time.

Monique Rona, the mother of one of Bill Gates's fellow students, was a founder of a Seattle-based business called Computer Center Corporation, also known as C-Cubed. The company did not make computers. Instead, C-Cubed bought computers. It then leased computer time to all sorts of businesses in the Pacific Northwest. C-Cubed would set up a connection between a computer in their office, such as the PDP-

10 that the Lakeside students used, and a particular business. The business then paid Computer Center Corporation a price for time on the computer.

Monique Rona was familiar with the computer the boys were using at Lakeside and she knew how enthusiastic they were about it. She also recognized how smart they were. So she made the school an offer.

Since computers were still very much in the experimental stage, they were often breaking down, or crashing. People were needed to check for problems, or bugs, in the computers. These bugs could either be in the actual machinery, known as hardware, or the programs, known as software. Instead of paying a professional person to do the job, Rona and the other C-Cubed staff decided to allow the computer-savvy Lakeside boys to try their hands at it. The boys would not get paid money. However, they would be paid in all the free computer time they wanted.

Gates, Allen, Weiland, and Evans spent their time after company hours trying their best to crash the computers at C-Cubed. The people at C-Cubed not only permitted the boys to try to cause problems on their computers, they encouraged them. That was the best way to ensure that their machinery would not fail when used by businesses.

By constantly experimenting, the Lakeside Programmers Group had no trouble finding ways to make the computer crash. For example, Gates wrote a program in the BASIC language he called Bill. Yet every time he tried to load his program, the PDP-10 computer crashed.

This happened several times and, at first, Gates could not figure out the problem. By way of the teletype machine, the computer asked, "NEW OR OLD [PROGRAM]."

Gates typed in, "OLD."

The teletype machine then punched out, "OLD PROGRAM NAME."

Gates would answer, "OLD PROGRAM NAME BILL."

Every time Gates punched in that response, the computer crashed.

With the help of a professional programmer at C-Cubed, Gates learned what was making the computer crash. The words, "OLD PROGRAM NAME BILL," were too much for the computer to process. When asked the name of the old program, he should have typed in simply "BILL."[2]

The quartet of boys was spending as much time as possible at C-Cubed. They often worked until midnight on weekdays and on weekends, too. They lived on a diet of pizza, soft drinks, and junk food. Gates commonly took his C-Cubed work home with him. His bedroom, usually messy with dirty clothes and books, now was even more cluttered with computer punch cards and scattered pieces of computer paper.

Although his work at C-Cubed may have been his primary interest, Gates and the other members of the Lakeside Programmers Group were still full-time students. Gates's teachers pushed him to be active in subjects that were not technical in nature. To his English teacher, Ann Stephens, getting A's was not enough. She did not like the fact that he sat in back of the classroom and rarely participated in discussions. One day she told him, "Bill, you're just coasting. Here are my ten favorite books; read these."[3]

Gates said, "She challenged me to do more. I never would have come to enjoy literature as much as I do if she hadn't pushed me."[4]

Stephens was not the only person to encourage Gates to explore other interests. His parents began to think their son was spending too much time in the computer room at McAllister Hall. Then there was one incident that made his parents think he had gone off the deep end.

By late 1969, C-Cubed was having financial problems. The company finally went out of business in March 1970. Knowing that C-Cubed was desperate for any money it could get, Bill Gates and Kent Evans purchased DEC computer tapes at bargain prices from the owners of C-Cubed. Although some of these tapes were blank, others contained computer program data. The boys first hid the tapes in the base of the teletype machine. Then they sold them for a hearty profit.

There was one problem with this deal. The boys' other business partners from the Lakeside Programmers Group, Paul Allen and Richard Weiland, were angry not to be part of the arrangement. After all, they had worked alongside Gates and Evans as a team. The four boys had a fierce argument over the matter. There are different versions of the details of what happened. Some historians say Allen discovered the tapes and took them for himself. Others say that Gates and Evans threatened to retain a lawyer and go to court to keep the tapes. That was despite the fact that they were just in ninth grade. The four boys eventually resolved the problem, although there are different versions, too, of how that was accomplished.

This incident convinced Mary and Bill Gates, Jr., that their son was too obsessed with computers. They ordered him to take a break from the computer lab. So from the end of ninth grade through the first half of tenth grade, Gates pursued other interests. That included literature, as Ann Stephens had suggested. He read biographies of Franklin Roosevelt and Napoléon, as well as perennial teenage favorites *A Separate Peace* and *The Catcher in the Rye*. He also read business and science books, and he spent time on science and math projects—ones that did not involve computers.

While Bill Gates was on his forced vacation from computers, Paul Allen was discovering different computers on the campus at the University of Washington

Bill Gates and Paul Allen sit courtside at a basketball game between the Portland Trailblazers and Seattle Supersonics in Seattle on March 11, 2003. Allen purchased the Trailblazers franchise in 1988.

(UW) in Seattle. Allen's father worked there, so it was easy for Paul to explore campus buildings. One computer was in the university's physics department building. Another was in UW's hospital. When Bill Gates was halfway through tenth grade, he joined Allen in experimenting with just about any computer they could get their hands on. Gates's break from computers did nothing to lessen his fascination with them.

Nor did it decrease his interest in earning money from computers. He did not have to look hard for his next job. Information Systems Incorporated (ISI) was a Portland, Oregon, based computer time-sharing company similar to C-Cubed. ISI's president, Tom McLain, needed someone to write a payroll program for one of its clients. Since ISI was headquartered in Portland, it needed a representative in Seattle to keep contacts with its Seattle customers. The Seattle representative, Frank Peep, had worked for C-Cubed before it went out of business, and he knew all about the Lakeside Programmers Group.

Peep hired the boys to write the payroll program for ISI. However, Peep insisted it be written in a language called Common Business-Oriented Language (COBOL). COBOL was the programming language used by most businesses at the time. The experience was valuable, and not just because the boys used a computer language other than BASIC. It was also the first time they worked in a professional business environment. They were rewarded with both free computer time as well as royalties, or a percentage of the profits ISI made.

When Bill Gates was halfway through tenth grade, he joined Allen in experimenting with just about any computer they could get their hands on.

Gates began to wonder what kind of program he could design on his own. In the summer between his sophomore and junior years, Allen showed Gates an article from a recent edition of *Electronics* magazine. Although Allen had graduated from Lakeside and was a freshman at Washington State University, the two stayed in close touch.

The article described a new product called a microprocessor chip that had been released by a company called Intel. The microprocessor is a small chip that is basically the brain of a computer. Intel called this chip the 8008. By today's standards, it was a tiny thing. But Gates and Allen recognized it as the key to the way of the future.

Gates and Allen purchased an 8008 microprocessor and used it to design a program that analyzed the amount of traffic on city streets. City engineers use that kind of information to decide how long traffic lights should be red, yellow, or green to keep traffic flowing as smoothly as possible.

You may have been in a car when you felt a bump as the car crossed a rubber hose in the street. As a car crossed over the hose, a paper tape in a box at the end of the hose was punched. Gates and Allen designed a computer program that would analyze the data more quickly and cheaply than had been done previously. They organized their first company around this program and called it Traf-O-Data.

The program actually worked and a few towns purchased it. However, Gates said that "no one actually wanted to buy the machine, at least not from a couple of teenagers."[5] Still, it is estimated that Gates and Allen grossed about twenty thousand dollars from Traf-O-Data.[6]

Although Kent Evans was not part of the Traf-O-Data company, Gates continued to work together with Evans on other projects. Tragically, their working relationship and friendship ended on May 28, 1972. While hiking on a mountaineering trip, Evans tripped and fell eight hundred feet. He died while on board a rescue helicopter. Gates was devastated at the death of his best friend and cried openly at Evans's funeral.[7]

But as hard as it was for Gates, life went on. Gates spent much of that summer in Washington, D.C. An old friend of his parents, Brock Adams, was now a Democratic member of the House of Representatives. Adams recommended Bill to be a congressional page for the summer. Gates was selected and served from July 17 to August 18, 1972.

Congressional pages deliver legislative documents to offices of the members of Congress. They may also bring new bills and amendments to the House floor or perform basic clerical jobs. Although the work is routine, many members of the Senate and House of Representatives started out as congressional pages. Experience as a page is a big boost for college graduates trying to be accepted into law school. At this time, Gates did not know what he wanted to do for a career.

In the fall of 1972, Gates entered his senior year

of high school and right away he again began to play with his favorite toys: computers. He and Paul Allen were assigned to schedule classes for the students at Lakeside. Lakeside had by then merged with the all-girls St. Nicholas School, and Gates went out of his way to arrange to be in classes with a lot of girls and few boys. On top of that, he and Allen were paid $4,200 for their work.[8]

Still, his teachers tried to make sure Gates's life extended beyond the world of computers. Ann Stephens, the English teacher, encouraged Gates to sign up for drama. She assigned him the lead role in a school play, a romantic comedy. When he was fifty years old, Gates went back to Lakeside to speak to the current Lakeside students. He said the only downside of playing the lead was "that I invited my co-star to our real-life prom, and she turned me down. She's here tonight, and I want her to know: I recently got over it."[9]

Regardless of his adventures in acting, the technical world always seemed to be calling to Gates. In the middle of his senior year, that proved to be literally true. One day, he received a phone call from a representative of a huge defense contracting business called TRW. It had been trying to computerize power grids in the Pacific Northwest and had problems with bugs in their computers. TRW employees had scanned a problem report book that had been kept by the defunct company C-Cubed. In the book, they repeatedly found the names of Gates and Allen as master bug repairers.

TRW wanted these two young men to save their new computer system. Allen and Gates accepted right away. Unlike their business, Traf-O-Data, this would be a salaried job at a well-known company. They would be paid $165 a week.[10] Many college graduates starting their careers in the early 1970s were not making that much money.

Allen decided to temporarily leave Washington State and Gates was given a leave of absence from Lakeside. That meant he could return to Lakeside to graduate without being penalized. The two moved to Vancouver, Washington, about one hundred sixty miles south of Seattle, to take the job for TRW. They worked there for about three months. Gates returned to Lakeside in the early spring of his senior year to finish high school.

After graduation, Gates and Allen returned to Vancouver to work on more projects with TRW. Gates used some of the money he earned to buy a speedboat, and he had fun water-skiing on the lakes of the Pacific Northwest.

In the fall, Gates left the Northwest to take a three-thousand-mile trip east. He was starting a new life as a freshman at Harvard University in Cambridge, Massachusetts.

4

"WE HOPE NOT A TURKEY"

Many students arrive at college with their minds made up about their future careers. Bill Gates was not one of them.

When Gates arrived in Cambridge, Massachusetts, as a college freshman in fall 1973, he declared pre-law as his major. That meant he was going to take more courses in law than any other subject, with the intent of going to law school after he graduated. However, students can change their majors. Gates did not know if he really wanted to be a lawyer like his father.

Since he liked math, Gates thought about becoming a math teacher. Of course, he loved computers, so maybe he would do something with computers for a living. His parents put no pressure on him regarding a future career. However, they felt it was important that he go to college.

Sure, he would receive a high-quality education. But his parents also wanted their son exposed to people of other backgrounds.

That happened right away. Gates was assigned to live with two freshman roommates. One was Sam Znaimer, a young Jewish man from a poor family who lived in Montreal. Sam's parents were Holocaust survivors. Bill's other roommate was Jim Jenkins, an African American from Chattanooga, Tennessee. The three students from diverse backgrounds shared the same room their freshman year.

Even though Gates attended classes in a variety of subjects, such as literature, psychology, economics, and history, he soon discovered there was one place he could not stay away from: the university's computer lab. Harvard's Aiken Computer Center had a PDP-10 computer, and Bill spent many nights there. If he was not playing computer games, he was designing his own.

As he did at Lakeside, Gates worked hard mainly at the subjects he liked. Still, he earned good grades his freshman year in all his subjects. He was one of those rare students who was intelligent enough to do well without trying hard.

While Gates was in Cambridge, his old friend Paul Allen was back in Washington promoting their company Traf-O-Data. However, Allen had trouble interesting cities and towns in his product. Some

Bill Gates works on a network program with Booker T. Washington High School student Eli Philippe in July 2001. Gates was at the Miami school to announce a series of grants to South Florida students. In his college days, Gates spent most of his time in the computer lab.

communities were able to get the federal government to analyze traffic patterns as a free service. So the boys let Traf-O-Data die a quiet death. They did not give up, though, and began to look for other projects.

In the summer of 1974, after Gates's freshman year had ended, Allen moved to Boston and took a job at the Honeywell company. But his main reason for moving east was to work closely with Gates on new ideas.

Gates and Allen avidly read magazines about electronics. They knew computers were going to be the key to the future. However, many experts thought computers would be used only by businesses. Even though computers were smaller than ever before, no one had yet created a handy and reliable personal computer.

In addition, the notion that average citizens would ever want computers for personal use was hard for many experts to believe. If that ever did happen, they thought, personal computers would be used by relatively few people—only those who were technically minded. As late as 1977, Ken Olson, founder of Digital Equipment Corporation said, "There is no reason anyone would want a computer in their home."[1]

Bill Gates and Paul Allen felt the opposite. They felt computers were the way of the future. They felt computers would change the way everyday people lived. They saw computers as the keystone of a technological revolution—the way the printing press, the automobile, and the airplane had been in past times.

Both Gates and Allen wanted to be part of this trend. But Allen seemed to be the driving force.

Gates said, "Paul kept saying, 'Let's start a company, let's do it.' Paul saw that the technology was there. He kept saying, 'It's gonna be too late. We'll miss it.'"[2]

They just were not sure of the best way to take part in the upcoming computer revolution.

So in the fall of 1974, Gates went back to Harvard and Allen kept working at Honeywell. At college, Gates found a new activity to occupy his spare time. He continued to spend a lot of time in the computer lab. But he also made many visits to a spare room in his new dormitory, Currier Hall. It was called the poker room, and on any evening there was also a lively game of poker taking place.

Gates loved the game, and he and his friends took it very seriously. His attitude toward poker was not much different than his attitude toward the games of go fish and bridge that he played with his grandmother ten years earlier. Playing poker was another way to use one's brains and strategic abilities. There were games in which players won or lost hundreds, or even more than a thousand dollars a night.

One of Gates's new friends who lived down the hall from him was a burly young man from Detroit, Steve Ballmer. While Gates was shy and reserved, Ballmer was outgoing and gregarious. The two complimented each other. Ballmer said the poker games were very intense, but there were other activities that were just as intense. That included friendly discussions. He said of Gates, "He'd play poker until 6 in the morning, then I'd run into him at breakfast and discuss applied mathematics."[3]

It was on a December night that year when Paul Allen came across the January issue of *Popular Electronics* that featured Ed Roberts's Altair 8080 on its cover. After Roberts was convinced that Gates's and Allen's BASIC system worked, he lured Allen away from Honeywell to work for him. Gates stayed in Cambridge to finish his sophomore year at Harvard.

As soon as the spring semester was over, Gates headed to Albuquerque to join his friend. The system may have worked on a test run, but it was hardly ready to be sold to the public. There were bugs to be removed. That did not matter to Ed Roberts. He was in a rush to sell his Altair to customers, especially before some competitor started selling his or her own microcomputer. Roberts advertised the Altair and took orders, even though the software to run the machine was not ready. Some frustrated customers called the MITS offices, wondering where their computers were. They were told the computers were on back order.

Roberts spent the summer of 1975 touring the country in a blue mobile home he called the MITS-Mobile. He stopped in cities and towns where he set up demonstrations showing potential customers how to

Microsoft began as strictly a software company. By 1984, Gates had made the cover of *Time* magazine (above), due to the growing success of the company.

use the Altair. He suggested that some of the computer fanatics that flocked to his MITS-Mobile start their own computer clubs. One group that did so was called the Homebrew Computer Club. It was based around Menlo Park, California, about an hour south of San Francisco. Menlo Park is also very close to Stanford University, where professors and other scientists were at the forefront of exploring the latest in computer technology. Members of the Homebrew Computer Club included a couple of electronic brainiacs named Steve Wozniak and Steve Jobs.

Sometimes Gates joined Roberts on the road in the MITS-Mobile. Other times, he worked closely with Allen trying to perfect their BASIC program. During the summer, they developed an 8K program, but they soon realized they could not do all the work themselves.

Gates contacted a younger Lakeside student named Chris Larson to help him out. He also called his friend Monte Davidoff from Harvard. The four of them spent the rest of the summer living together in the same apartment and working together at MITS. When fall arrived, Gates and Davidoff returned to Harvard and Larson went back to Lakeside in Seattle. Allen stayed in Albuquerque to continue working on software for the Altair.

However, Allen needed help with new projects Roberts wanted to introduce. At the end of the fall semester, Gates flew back to Albuquerque to work with Allen. One of Roberts's new ideas was a floppy-disk storage system for his Altair. This would replace the paper tape system. The data would be stored on a magnetic disk, known as a floppy disk, or simply a floppy. Gates was given the assignment to come up with a version of BASIC that would work with a floppy disk. He virtually locked himself in the MITS software lab to work on this new job. Just five days later, Gates introduced to Roberts and the rest of the MITS staff a software system that worked with floppy disks.

Although Gates and Allen did work for Roberts and his MITS company, they were not employed by MITS. They ran their own business developing software. They made money by allowing Roberts the right to use their software.

Up until now, Gates's and Allen's business did not have a name. Because they were designing microcomputer software, they combined the beginnings of both words and called it Micro-Soft. Shortly afterward, the hyphen was dropped, and the company name became all one word: Microsoft.

Gates considered dropping out of college to devote full time to Microsoft. His parents were not happy with that idea.[4] The Gates family Christmas card for 1975 included a photograph of the three Gates children. A short poem about each child accompanied the photo. Bill, Jr., and Mary wrote the following poem about their son, Bill, or Trey:

Trey took time off this fall
　　in old Albuquerque
His own software business—
　　We hope not a turkey.
　　(The profits are murky.)[5]

Gates did return to Harvard for the spring semester of his junior year, but his heart was not in his college studies. He was concerned mostly about his business. He was especially upset to learn that some computer users were using but not paying for the BASIC software he designed for the Altair. Many computer hobbyists were making copies of their friends' original software. It is similar to making copies of friends' compact discs, or downloading music today from the Internet without paying for it.

This type of thing has become a very heated issue. To some users, this practice is harmless sharing, like lending your lawnmower to your neighbor next door. To others, especially software manufacturers, it is outright stealing. This practice has become known as software piracy.

Gates falls into the second category. He has always believed sharing software is stealing. He put his views in words in a famous open letter he wrote shortly after

Gates reclines on his desk in this publicity photo taken shortly after Microsoft's release of Windows 1.0 in November 1985.

his BASIC software went on sale. It appeared in the February 1976 issue of *Computer Notes*, a newsletter published by MITS. A staff member at MITS sent a copy to every computer publication he could find. Titled simply, "An Open Letter to Hobbyists," it has become legendary in computer history.

Gates expressed his outrage at what he considered the theft of his work. He wrote: "As the majority of hobbyists must be aware, most of you steal your software." He then continued writing from the point of view of those he considered software-stealers. "Hardware must be paid for, but software is something to share. Who cares if the people who worked on it don't get paid?"

Gates finished the letter from his own point of view. He added: "What hobbyist can put three man years into programming, finding all bugs, documenting his product and distribute for free. The fact is, no one besides us has invested a lot of money in hobby software. . . . Most directly, the thing you do is theft."[6]

Gates concluded the open letter by asking for people to pay him. He said he would accept suggestions or comments, too. He included his address in New Mexico for hobbyists to either send him money or suggestions.

Some of Gates's fellow programmers at other software companies defended Gates. However, many users responded in a way Gates did not have in mind. One was Lee Felsenstein, a member of the Homebrew Computer Club in California, which was then meeting in the Stanford Linear Accelerator Center (SLAC) auditorium on the Stanford University campus.

Felsenstein said, "I read it aloud from the floor of the Homebrew Computer Club. To great derision. I read it to the multitudes assembled in the SLAC auditorium. Everybody thought that was hilarious, and they were damned if they were going to send them $500."[7]

A few hobbyists did send Gates money for his BASIC software. Most did not. Many objected to being called thieves. They responded by sending Gates angry letters. Others said that copying software was no different than taping music off the radio or from other people's record albums. Some critics who had to wait longer than expected for their computers to arrive said it was hypocritical for Altair or Gates to accuse anyone of unfair practices. They accused Altair of "misleading advertising and failure to deliver mail order products as advertised in a reasonable time."[8]

Gates has refused to let go of the issue of piracy, and it is a controversial topic to this day.

As for Bill Gates's future, it was not going to be at Harvard.

5
LONG DAYS IN THE DESERT

In 1976, **Microsoft moved** to its first official office. It was located on the eighth floor of a bank building near Albuquerque's airport. The address made the location sound ritzy: Two Park Central Tower. However, it was merely a nondescript office building like many others in cities across the nation. Still, the office location helped cement the idea that these young people were not mere computer hobbyists. Microsoft meant business.

When Gates and Allen were not actually working on computer programming, they were putting their efforts into hiring programmers to work for Microsoft. Some they hired were those they had worked with before, such as Rick Weiland and Chris Larson. Others were new discoveries who knew their way around computers. These included a married couple, Steve and Marla Wood.

However, one new employee was a forty-two year old woman named Miriam Lubow, who knew absolutely nothing about computers. She was hired as an office manager, in charge of duties such as organizing files, making sure the workers were paid on time, and purchasing necessary supplies.

Since Lubow was roughly twice as old as the other Microsoft employees, she also became a protective mother hen to Gates and the rest of the staff. Gates had acquired a bad habit of waiting until the last minute to catch airplane flights. To make sure he did not miss important flights, Lubow would tell Gates that his flights' estimated departure times were earlier than they actually were. That way she made certain he would be at the airport on time.

In fact, Lubow was shocked when she first met Gates. She had been hired while he was away on business. When he returned to work, Lubow was sitting at her desk when a young man with a head full of long, uncombed, reddish-blond hair and wearing jeans walked past her into Gates's office. Lubow thought some teenager had entered Gates' office and she called Steve Wood. Wood told her that was not some teenager, but the company owner.

When she got to know Gates, she realized he was as serious as one can be about work. Gates and the rest may have dressed like slobs and lived on a diet of soft drinks and pizza. But they lived and breathed computers.

A full-time job is officially forty hours a week, but Gates and the staff often worked eighty to ninety hours a week.

Lubow said, "I could tell this guy was different and that he was going places. For him, his work was always a quest for knowledge, something he was doing because he loved it."[1]

Gates's long hours did not leave him much time for a social life. In the little free time he had he liked going to movies. Sometimes he would work a long day, then leave the office for a movie. After the movie, he would go back to the office and go right back to work.

> **Gates and the rest may have dressed like slobs and lived on a diet of soft drinks and pizza. But they lived and breathed computers.**

Aside from movies, Gates loved fast cars. Not long after arriving in Albuquerque, he bought a green Porsche 911, an expensive and fast sports car. To let off steam after a long day at work Gates liked to take his Porsche on a fast spin on the desert roads of central New Mexico. Many times he broke the speed limit, and many times the police caught him and punished him with speeding fines.

Just as Lakeside School had to lease computer time

years earlier, Microsoft did as well during its first years in business. In a reversal of his school days, Gates arranged for Microsoft to lease computer time from computers in Albuquerque's public-school system. Since Microsoft had no printers in its offices, every day a Microsoft employee had to make a trip to the Albuquerque public-school administration building to get printouts.

As a business owner, Gates had to do more than program computers to make decent money. He could not rely on selling Microsoft software only through Altair purchases. He had to look for more customers to buy his software.

While technical whizzes know their way around the wires and microchips inside a computer, many do not have business skills. They are able to work wonders with computers, but they need to work for someone else to make a living. What makes Gates different from most is his business sense. He is a skilled computer programmer but also a talented businessman.

Gates made sales calls to some of the best-known businesses in the world, convincing people twice his age that they need Microsoft software for their companies to thrive in the coming high-tech world. In 1976, Microsoft made a deal with one of the largest companies in the United States: General Electric (GE). GE paid Microsoft and Altair together a total of fifty thousand dollars for the right to run Microsoft BASIC anywhere in its computer system.[2]

Microsoft then made a business agreement with another big corporation, National Cash Register (NCR). Microsoft developed a digital cassette BASIC that would work with NCR's computer system. A Microsoft programmer named Marc McDonald and Gates have both been credited by different computer historians with developing the stand-alone disk BASIC for NCR.

Near the end of 1976, Allen quit working for MITS so he could devote all his time to Microsoft. He could see that the future was not going to ride on the back of the Altair. Not long after MITS began selling its Altair, other businesses developed and began selling their own microcomputers.

> **What makes Gates different from most is his business sense. He is a skilled computer programmer but also a talented businessman.**

One such company was Commodore, which released its own microcomputer it called Personal Electronic Transactor, or PET. In northern California, Steve Wozniak and Steve Jobs—once members of the Homebrew Computer Club—introduced to the public their own personal computer, the Apple II. In Texas,

Steve Jobs introduces his new Apple II computer in 1977 (above).

the owners of the Radio Shack chain of stores, Tandy Corporation, came out with a microcomputer called the TRS-80.

Gates and Allen knew that Ed Roberts and his small Altair company would likely be left in the dust as more and more businesses were creating their own personal computers. In addition, Gates and Roberts had not been getting along for a while. It seemed they were constantly arguing.[3] Gates knew that the best business decision he could make was to separate himself from MITS to be free to sell Microsoft software to other microcomputer companies. Although they were not getting along, Roberts did not want Gates to leave MITS. He relied on Gates and the other Microsoft engineers to help him sell his Altair.

On May 22, 1977, Roberts, tired of the whole computer business, sold MITS to a company called Pertec. The staff at Pertec felt that their company therefore owned a fair share of Microsoft's BASIC software. Gates insisted that Pertec owned none of it. After a complex legal battle, an arbitrator, or person selected to settle the dispute, ruled that Microsoft's BASIC software belonged entirely to Microsoft. Gates was free to sell his software to whomever he wanted and Pertec had no legal right to any money from those sales.

Although the skinny, mop-haired Gates looked more like a high-school sophomore than a businessman, he held his own in the legal battle for exclusive

The first IBM personal computer (PC) was outfitted with a monitor, keyboard, printer, and Microsoft's MS-DOS software. Microsoft earned a royalty on every copy of the software.

rights to his software. In fact, because he looked so young, the lawyers for Pertec may have underestimated his intelligence and skill. As for Ed Roberts, he completely quit the computer business. He went to medical school, moved to Georgia, and became a family doctor.

Gates got busy right away selling Microsoft BASIC software to other computer manufacturers. He made a deal with Tandy to use his BASIC software in Tandy's TRS-80. Tandy would sell the TRS-80 in Radio Shack stores across the country and each one ran on Microsoft BASIC. For each TRS-80 that sold, Microsoft received a royalty, or percentage of the cost.

Gates also sold a version of BASIC to Apple to run

in its Apple II computer. Microsoft then made deals with Commodore. One of Gates' best decisions was to sell Microsoft to businesses beyond the United States borders. He made friends with a computer whiz kid from Japan, Kazuhiko Nishi, known by the nickname Kay. Nishi and Gates had much in common. Both were college students who spent more time on computer businesses than their college studies. Nishi and Gates signed a contract giving Nishi exclusive rights to distribute Microsoft software in east Asia. That meant there was no way any other person or company could sell Microsoft software in that highly populated part of the world.

Unlike the complicated dealings with Pertec, this business agreement was easy and friendly. Gates said, "There were no attorneys involved, just Kay and I, kindred spirits. We did more than $150 million of business under that contract—more than ten times what we had expected."[4] Gates, Allen, and the rest of the young computer nerds at Microsoft were on their way to setting the computer operating standards for the world.

With Microsoft growing, Gates officially dropped out of college in January 1977. Gates and Allen started to develop software in other computer languages to run as Microsoft products. One was FORTRAN, short for "formula transition." FORTRAN was developed in 1956 by a team of computer

Intel chairman Andy Grove and Bill Gates celebrate the twentieth anniversary of the personal computer in this publicity photo taken in 2001. At either end are two of the oldest PCs, while at center are three modern laptops.

technicians at another megacorporation, International Business Machines, (IBM). Another was a complicated language known by a simple name, "a programming language," or APL. A third was an obscure language called FOCAL.

However, none of the software programmed in these languages sold as well as Microsoft BASIC. FOCAL was a complete disaster. It was too complex for most users.

By the late 1970s, Gates felt that Microsoft needed to move from Albuquerque. Albuquerque is a fascinating city with its western, Latino, and American Indian influences, but in the world of high-tech business in

1978, it was a backwater. That summer, Gates began to look for a new company headquarters.

Northern California was becoming known as the high-tech capital of the nation, and Gates thought that might be the best place to relocate. Another possibility was the Dallas/Fort Worth area, where Tandy Corporation's world headquarters is located. However, Paul Allen favored moving Microsoft back to their home base, Seattle. When Bill, Jr., and Mary Gates heard that their son was planning on moving, they welcomed the opportunity for him to come back home. And so, in December 1979 and January 1980, the entire staff, with one exception, relocated to Seattle. The exception was Miriam Lubow. Her family was in Albuquerque, so she chose to stay.

On December 7, 1979, a Microsoft programmer named Bob Greenberg decided a photo should be taken of the entire Microsoft staff. Because a snowstorm hit the city that day, Lubow stayed home with her children. The other eleven posed for the company portrait.

That photograph has since become famous. It features nine young men and two young women who look more like 1960s-era hippies than businesspersons who would become among the richest in the world. With the exception of Gates and Greenberg, all the men have some sort of facial hair. Some of the men have shoulder-length long hair parted in the middle.

A large cut-out of a famous photograph taken of the Microsoft staff in December 1979 is shown here on display at the Microsoft Visitor Center in Redmond, Washington, on April 6, 2005. A young Bill Gates can be seen in the lower left corner while Paul Allen sits in the lower right.

Marla Wood has a forest of long, flowing black hair, and she wears vintage wire-rim glasses.

The full-color photo has since been featured in many magazines. It has also been the subject of a frequently sent e-mail. The caption accompanying the photo usually reads: "Look at them!!! Would you have invested in a company created by these people? (look at the guy in the lower left corner!!!)"[5]

The guy in the lower left corner is a skinny young man who looks sixteen years old. He has reddish-brown hair combed over his forehead, and he wears a blue button-down sport shirt open at the neck. A white undershirt is seen poking up. That guy in the lower left corner is Bill Gates.

6
DRESSING UP
FOR IBM

For decades, IBM had been one of the leaders in making mainframe computers. As the 1980s began, IBM executives decided to venture into the manufacture of personal computers. IBM was by now certain that personal computers were not a fad.

However, they needed someone to write the software for their personal computers. The people at IBM had heard promising things about Bill Gates and his still fairly new software company. So in July 1980, an IBM representative named Jack Sams called Microsoft's offices in Seattle to talk about doing business with them. Soon afterward, Sams and two other IBM officials flew to Seattle to discuss a possible software deal with Microsoft. Sams and his partners were impressed with Gates's honesty and competence. They decided Microsoft was the right company to design the operating software for their IBM personal computer, or IBM PC.

Almost immediately, Gates put his staff to work writing Microsoft programs for IBM. Microsoft's first priority was to design software for an operating system (OS) for the IBM PC. No computer can run without an OS. It is the software that controls a computer's basic operations.

Through the rest of summer and fall, Microsoft and IBM corresponded back and forth about this software project they called Operation Chess. The goings-on were kept totally secret as if this was an international spy arrangement. To get a running start on the project, Gates contacted a Seattle friend named Tim Paterson. Paterson was a computer engineer who owned a local business named Seattle Computer Products. Paterson had already designed his own operating system he called QDOS, which was an acronym for "quick and dirty operating system." Microsoft purchased QDOS from Paterson and used it as a basis for the system he would write for IBM.

Since they were a few years late entering into the personal computer market, IBM was in a rush to get theirs into stores. To speed up the manufacture of their personal computers, IBM executives decided not to make them from scratch. They would make them from parts of old computers.

By October 1980, a design for an operating system

Today, Microsoft continues to lead the computer industry in the development of many different software programs (such as Access, above).

for the IBM PC was ready. That month, Gates hopped aboard a nonstop flight to Miami for what was likely the most important business meeting in the history of Microsoft. With him were two other Microsoft staff members. One was a programmer from Texas named Bob O'Rear. The other was his old friend from Harvard, Steve Ballmer, who Gates had hired in June 1980. Ballmer did not know much about the inner workings of computers. However, he was an outgoing businessman who felt comfortable around people. With burly Steve Ballmer by his side, Gates could rest assured he was with someone who had sharp business skills.

The meeting with IBM was so important that Gates, Ballmer, and O'Rear ditched their usual casual wardrobes and dressed in business suits. Gates was so unused to dressing in business attire that he forgot to bring with him a necessary clothing item—a necktie. So when the men from Microsoft were driving from the airport to the IBM offices, they had to make an unscheduled stop at a department store to buy a necktie for the company head.

Such an ornamental piece of clothing might seem

like a small detail. However, IBM is a very traditional company. Gates and the others would be meeting with people who tended to be conservative and sticklers for tradition, and who were old enough to be their parents. For Gates to arrive at IBM in his usual business clothing—jeans, sneakers, and either a casual sport shirt or a well-worn sweater—would be as jarring as showing up with a Mohawk haircut.

At the meeting, Gates did most of the talking. Ballmer and O'Rear were on hand to provide support if necessary. About ten IBM executives and attorneys were on hand to listen to Gates's presentation. He not only explained how the operating system would work, but he also discussed the kind of business deal he expected.

Gates could have been paid a flat fee for selling the Microsoft system to IBM. But Gates had another idea. He was confident that the IBM PC would be a hot seller. So he asked to be paid by a royalty system. Instead of being given one big payment for selling software to IBM, Microsoft would get a portion of the money from the sale of every IBM PC with Microsoft software. So as long as his software sold, he would keep getting money. It was this type of thinking that helped him ultimately become the richest man in the world.

After Gates spoke to IBM's staff, he was peppered with questions from them. Most had to do with the operating system and how it would work. Although he

First Space Shuttle Mission

On April 12, 1981, at 7:00 A.M., NASA's Space Shuttle Program began with the launch of the *Columbia* from the Kennedy Space Center in Florida. Astronauts John Young and Robert Crippen were on a mission to demonstrate a safe launch into orbit, check the performance of the space shuttle's systems, and return safely to earth. The shuttle carried equipment that measured and recorded the temperatures, pressures, acceleration levels, and stresses during liftoff, the orbital flight, and landing. The *Columbia* landed at Edwards Air Force Base in California on April 14 1981. All mission objectives were met successfully. A post-flight inspection of the shuttle showed that the orbiter was damaged during the launch. Sixteen heat shield tiles were lost and 148 others were damaged due to an overpressure wave created by the solid rocket boosters.

The *Columbia* flew a total of twenty-eight missions. On February 1, 2003, it was destroyed while re-entering Earth's atmosphere. All seven astronauts aboard died in the disaster.

was not as socially skilled as Steve Ballmer, Gates held his own with the IBM people. He appeared poised and confident.

No final decision was made in Florida. Gates, Ballmer, and O'Rear flew back to Seattle. In the following days, Gates and representatives from IBM continued to discuss the possible deal over the phone. Finally, in early November, two representatives from IBM flew to Seattle. On November 6, 1980, they signed a contract with Gates and Ballmer.

Hard work had been completed, but harder work was to follow. IBM gave Microsoft a series of deadlines to meet in order to have a computer with a working operating system for sale as soon as possible. For the next nine months, it was work, work, work.

The only break they took was an early spring trip to Florida to see the first ever space shuttle takeoff on Sunday, April 12.

As tech-minded people, Paul Allen and several other fellow Microsoft programmers wanted to witness space history in the making. But Gates was concerned about being behind schedule and not meeting IBM's deadlines. Allen went to Florida, but he made sure the trip was as short as possible.

Gates said during an interview, "We worked day and night with this IBM machine in a back room. There were a lot of ups and downs. The one tiff Paul and I had was when he wanted to see a space shuttle launch and I didn't, because we were late. Still, these guys went to see the launch, and I was just . . . ."

Allen, also on hand for the interview, interrupted Gates and explained, "It was the first one, Bill. And we flew back the same day. We weren't gone even 36 hours."[1]

> **"We worked day and night with this IBM machine in a back room. There were a lot of ups and downs."**

Finally, on August 12, 1981, the IBM PC was introduced to the public. Being a huge company, IBM announced the arrival of its computer as part of a mega-event. The company rented a room in the famous Waldorf-Astoria Hotel in New York City and invited members of the major newspapers, magazines, and television networks. All the publicity worked. The IBM PC was a huge hit.

Since IBM had made its personal computers with parts from old computers, all sorts of computer-savvy people—professionals and amateurs alike—figured they could do the same thing. And they did. These computers became known as clones, and they were sold as cheaper competitors of the IBM PC.

That may have hurt IBM, but it did not hurt Microsoft. In the contract, IBM gave Microsoft permission to sell its MS-DOS operating system to other computer makers. So Microsoft did just that. There originally were two other official PC operating systems, but Microsoft soon left the others far behind.[2] Gates even sold some software programs to Microsoft's arch rival, Apple, in order to help some of Apple's early computers work sufficiently. These were smart decisions on Gates's part. With more and more businesses buying computers to help get their work done quicker and easier, the money started rolling in at Microsoft headquarters.

But it was not like Bill Gates to take it easy. As soon as MS-DOS became the standard operating system for the majority of personal computers, Gates came up with other ideas for Microsoft. In 1982, Microsoft came out with a spreadsheet program. It was called Multiplan. Spreadsheets allow computer users to keep track of finances, and they are used by both businesses and families. Thanks to spreadsheets, individuals could keep track of their family finances. That meant computers were becoming popular in people's homes, and they were not seen only as office equipment. In time, having a computer in your home would be as automatic as having a telephone or television set.

Then in 1983, Microsoft introduced a word-processing software program simply called Microsoft Word. The system that enabled Word to work was WYSIWYG (pronounced "wizzy-wig"). It stood for "what you see is what you get," a tagline of a then-popular comedian named Flip Wilson. In the case of Word, that was accurate. Words typed on a keyboard would appear on a computer monitor exactly as they would

In addition to software, Microsoft also develops many different kinds of computer hardware, such as this wireless laser mouse.

appear when printed on paper. It was the basis for most word-processing systems used since.

Gates lived and breathed computer programming so much that he did not have much time for leisure activities. He still liked going to movies and playing games, such as bridge and chess. In 1983, he bought a house not far from his parents' home. It had an indoor swimming pool, so sometimes he invited friends over to go swimming. Much of the time when he was not at his office, he would take his work home by reading computer and business publications.

Gates also did not have much time for dating. But in 1983, he attended a party held by Microsoft's director of design and production services, Tricia McGinnis. In attendance was a tall blonde sales representative for a different computer company. Her name was Jill Bennett. She and Gates started talking computers at the party, and before long they were seeing each other socially.

There was also some bad news in 1983. Gates's friend and Microsoft cofounder, Paul Allen, was told by a doctor that he had cancer. Luckily, it was a treatable form of cancer called Hodgkin's disease. However, it was severe enough for Allen to stop working full-time at Microsoft. Allen attended company meetings now and then but did not work full-time.

> The **money** started **rolling in** at **Microsoft headquarters. But it was not like** Bill Gates to take it **easy.**

Gates said, "It was terrible when Paul got sick. Nobody talked about work or anything; it was just a matter of wondering, Was Paul going to be okay? . . . It was really sad to go by his office, because all the memos and magazines would be stacked in there."[3]

The fact that Gates could not talk about work proved that he took Allen's illness very hard, since

Gates's life was his work. In fact, that is said to be a reason why he and Jill Bennett broke up. She had trouble dealing with the long hours he spent at work.

Then an event early in 1984 put a sense of shock into Gates and the rest of the employees at Microsoft. It started with of all things, a Super Bowl commercial on January 22, 1984. It was not something that Gates would take lightly.

7

"IT'S ALL ABOUT THE GOOEY"

There were a few ads for personal computers that ran during that Super Bowl telecast. One was for Radio Shack's personal computer. Another was for a computer manufactured by Atari, which was best known for making some of the earliest computer game software.

The commercial that blew people away, though, was for the new Macintosh computer made by Apple. It was a professionally filmed ad, directed by highly regarded movie director Ridley Scott.

The ad featured masses of bald-headed, look-alike, marching worker drones. They are escorted by guards resembling storm troopers, and they sit and listen to orders barked at them by an impersonal talking head on a giant screen. The scene is gray and dim. Interspersed are shots of a renegade—a young women with short-cropped blonde hair, running toward the big screen. She is wearing a bright red pair of shorts and a white exercise shirt. At the end of the commercial, she throws a sledgehammer toward the big screen, smashing it to pieces.

The big head is gone, and the drones sit stunned, with their mouths wide open. A voice says, "On January 24, Apple Computer will introduce Macintosh. And you'll see why 1984 won't be like *1984*."[1]

The reference was to the famous novel *1984* by George Orwell. It is about a future society in which people are unable to think freely and are forced to conform. The point of the ad was that users of IBM personal computers were like the drones in both the commercial and the society in the book, *1984*.

The message of the ad was that to think and act differently, computer users should switch from IBM personal computers to the new Macintosh.

The Macintosh, or Mac for short, was truly unlike any of the other personal computers then for sale to the public. To use the IBM and other personal computers, users had to type in commands. To some nontechnical people, this was a cumbersome and sometimes annoying process.

On the other hand, the Macintosh made use of a system called the graphical user interface, or GUI. Computer technicians sounded out GUI and referred to it as the "gooey." Instead of typing in commands, computer users controlled the computer with an attachment called a mouse. With the mouse in hand, they pointed to images on the computer screen. They then clicked the mouse to open them. This was a lot easier than familiarizing oneself with lengthy commands.

Technical writer Kevin Maney said, "The Mac made computing truly personal. It made an inaccessible process human."[2]

Maney compared the arrival of the Mac to the inventions of the telephone and the Kodak camera. Before Alexander Graham Bell's telephone was invented, people sent messages by way of the less convenient telegraph. Before George Eastman invented the Kodak camera, photography was an unwieldy process only professionals had the time and patience to work with.

The Macintosh, or Mac for short, was truly unlike any of the other personal computers then for sale to the public.

A Mac user named Peter Cochrane said that using the Mac instead of a computer programmed for MS-DOS "was like the difference between a ballpoint pen and a hammer and chisel."[3]

Since the Mac did not use the MS-DOS,

The Macintosh (or Mac) personal computer released by Apple in 1984.

Microsoft now had real competition. True, Gates and Apple had worked together a few years earlier, but that did not erase the fact that the two companies were rivals looking for the same customers.

Gates was determined not to let a competitor have an edge on Microsoft. He made developing a mouse-driven software system a top priority for the software engineers at Microsoft.

It was not as easy as Gates had hoped. He and his staff struggled for most of 1984 and well into 1985 trying to design an easy system that worked. Bugs would commonly show up. When some experimental systems did work, Gates often felt he could make better ones. He demanded that software engineers scrap programs they had been working on for weeks, as he felt a better system was just around the corner.

While Gates could be easygoing, he was also known for having a temper. That temper showed itself when things at work were frustrating him. One Microsoft programmer, Leo Nikora, said, "There were shouting matches all the time."[4] Gates was not above pounding his fist on a worker's desk to show his aggravation on the slow progress being made on the GUI project.

Gates did have some pleasant distractions from the agony of the GUI software project. At a business meeting in the spring of 1984, he met a beautiful, brainy software programmer named Ann Winblad. She was

Bill Gates grasps the hand of visually impaired ten-year-old Timothy Peters after the two played an online game against each other via the Children's Discovery Portal—the world's first internet portal for visually impaired or blind children. Microsoft originally struggled to come up with a workable GUI (Graphics-User Interface) system in the early 1980s.

based at a Minneapolis, Minnesota, company called Open Systems, Inc. Like Gates, she had a head for business and was a self-made millionaire.

The two soon began a long-distance dating relationship. They went together to conferences and research trips in places as far away as Brazil and Africa. In 1985, she moved to northern California for business reasons. Her new home was not exactly around the corner from Seattle, but it was closer than Minneapolis— just a short flight away. The two got together on weekends and holidays.

They even went on high-tech "virtual dates." When in different cities, Gates and Winblad would drive to theaters hundreds of miles apart showing the same movie. They would then discuss the movies on their cell phones.[5]

Winblad, a strict vegetarian, cared deeply for Gates. She was concerned about his health, especially his steady diet of hamburgers and soft drinks. Winblad persuaded Gates to give up meat.

Although Gates was a millionaire businessman, he still had a lot of little kid in him. He represented a new kind of businessman. He did not conform to accepted business standards and go to work in suits and ties like the executives at conservative, traditional IBM. Gates often arrived at work in casual and even messy clothes, like well-worn sweaters with holes or stains.

His office was usually a pigsty, just as his bedroom

had been when he was a child. Gates even kept his habit of rocking back and forth, like he did on his rocking horse as a toddler. Rocking on a chair at work became a Gates trademark. His employees knew that if the boss was rocking back and forth in his office, he was deep in thought.

His personal image was that of a nerd who became a millionaire. Young computer nerds across the world could not help but admire him. He was not a star athlete, rock star, or playboy businessman like Donald Trump. Published photos of Gates always showed a skinny, non-macho man with unkempt hair, horn-rim glasses, and mismatched or shabby clothes. If Bill Gates could do it, younger computer nerds thought, why could they not do the same if they work hard and use their brains?

> Young **computer nerds across** the **world** could not help **but admire** him.

In fact, even non-nerds respected Gates. To them he was an underdog who made good. Of course, that image did not take into account that he was from a very comfortable family background. The general public saw a man who did not become successful based on shallow factors such as physical appearance and charm. They viewed Gates as a person who did well because he was intelligent and worked hard.

Photos like this one (taken in 1990) often seemed to capture Gates as being small in stature with overly-large glasses, reinforcing the "computer nerd" stereotype with which he was labeled in Microsoft's early years.

Microsoft's GUI-based software was finally released to the public on November 21, 1985. Gates called the program Windows because the separate frames that appeared on the screen could be viewed as a kind of window with views of words and images. The software was officially called Windows 1.0. Although it was a relief to release a final product, it was not perfect. Many hardware companies were making computers that were too slow or lacked enough memory to use it.

Regardless of Windows' imperfections, Microsoft made enemies by releasing it. Apple accused Microsoft of stealing their idea. Stealing an idea like this is a type of copyright violation. After all, Apple was the company that originally used the GUI system.

However, Microsoft had been developing software for Apple for a few years. Microsoft's software programs, Excel and Word, enabled Apple's Mac to work. If Apple went ahead and sued Microsoft for copyright violation, Gates said he would stop developing

The general **public** saw a **man** who did **not become successful based on shallow factors** such as physical appearance and **charm**. They viewed Gates as a **person who did well** because he was **intelligent** and **worked hard**.

software for the Mac. Knowing how much it needed Microsoft's software, Apple dropped the lawsuit. The pressure Gates put on Apple proved to the general public that Gates was not only a skilled software engineer, but he could also be a tough businessman when necessary.

In late 1985 and early 1986, Gates made another sharp business decision. Until then, Microsoft had been a privately held company. That means that only Microsoft employees could own stock in Microsoft. A stock is a share of the company. When someone owns a share of a stock, that means he or she owns a portion of the company. If the company makes money, the shareholder makes money, too. If the company loses money, so does the shareholder.

Gates gave much thought about whether Microsoft should become a publicly held company. The financial risks could be great. What if the general public was not interested in buying stock in his company?

Gates had discussions with stock-market experts. After much consideration, he decided to go ahead with it. On the morning of March 13, 1986, Microsoft stock was for the first time publicly traded at the New York Stock Exchange. That means that people who do not work for Microsoft could now buy stock in the company. In a privately held company, stock owners cannot sell their shares. In a publicly held company, they can.

Microsoft's chief financial officer, Frank Gaudette, was at the stock exchange that morning. Gaudette called one of Microsoft's executives, John Shirley, and yelled, "It's wild! I've never seen anything like it—every last person here is trading Microsoft and nothing else."[6]

The morning of March 13, Microsoft's price per share was $25.75. When the day was over, the sale price had risen to $27.75.[7] Millions of Microsoft shares were sold that one day.

Gates made another big business decision that year. He moved Microsoft's headquarters to an expansive industrial park in Redmond, Washington, a Seattle suburb. His company was growing and it needed as much space as he could get.

Life was going well for Gates. He was still dating Ann Winblad off and on. However, Ann is five years older than Bill, and she was ready to settle down. Gates was not ready to do so. He was still very much involved in his work. He had also gone back to eating hamburgers, despite Winblad's attempt to turn him into a vegetarian. The two stopped dating, but they remain friends to this day.

Gates had loved games since he was a child, so he decided to plan a day of fun and games for the people who work at Microsoft. The event is called the Microgames, and it takes place at Cheerio, the

Bill Gates and Melinda French applaud as they sit courtside during a basketball game in Seattle on March 23, 1993.

Gates family's old summer camp. At the 1987 Microgames, Bill Gates met a dark-haired, twenty-three-year old Microsoft employee named Melinda French.

Like Bill, she is very intelligent and loves math. She graduated as valedictorian of her high school, Ursuline Academy in Dallas, Texas. French then graduated from college with degrees in both computer science and economics. At the time of the 1987 Microgames, she had recently joined Microsoft to work as a product unit manager. Soon, Bill and Melinda were dating.

Microsoft was still releasing a variety of software programs, but its best-selling item was Windows. In October 1987, an advanced version, Windows 2.03, was released. But Gates branched out beyond software programs. That year, Microsoft released its first CD-ROM, called Bookshelf. It was a collection of reference works, including a dictionary, thesaurus, and zip-code directory. Microsoft also continued producing spreadsheets and other varied software programs. It was also in 1987 that, thanks in great part to Microsoft going public, Bill Gates became the youngest millionaire in American history.

A total of four years after introducing the Macintosh, Microsoft's rival, Apple, was not doing as well as hoped. Most computer users were flocking to Microsoft's Windows software.

Then, on March 17, 1988, Apple sued Microsoft again for stealing some of Microsoft's features in its Windows 2.03 software. Apple said that Microsoft was allowed to use some Macintosh features in Windows 1.0 but not in Windows 2.03. Almost immediately, Microsoft sued Apple for breaking their agreement. Microsoft said that the features in Windows 2.03 were nearly identical to those used in Windows 1.0. A court ruled in March 1989 that the 1985 agreement between Apple and Microsoft did not fully apply to Windows 2.03.

However, nothing conclusive was decided. More questions were raised about the ethics of designing new technology. Is the act of developing computer technology like that of writing an article or screenplay in which all the material is assumed to be original? Or is it like building a better machine that improves on technology that was used before? To this day, people are still trying to come up with definite answers to these questions.

Not satisfied to stick solely to software and other computer-related products, Gates started a new company in 1989. It is called Corbis Corporation and is an archive of digital photographs and other historic images. Corbis employees use computer scanners to convert old photos into digital form. Gates was looking ahead to the future. He said, "I believe that quality images will be in great demand on the interactive network [today known as the Internet]. My idea that the public will find image-browsing a worthwhile pursuit remains to be demonstrated, but I think with the right interface the service will appeal to a lot of people. I'm looking forward to being able to ask for 'sailboats' or 'volcanoes' or 'famous scientists' and then seeing what turns up."[8]

While Gates was exploring other business projects such as Corbis, Microsoft programmers kept as busy as ever. On May 22, 1990, Microsoft introduced the newer and improved Windows 3.0 as part of a splashy presentation in New York City. The event was simulcast in thirteen cities around the world. Those not in New York watched the event on big-screen televisions.

Some observers thought it was all a bit too much. One magazine reporter wrote: "For this kind of fanfare, you'd expect software that will solve the S&L crisis and butter your toast in the morning."[9] (*S&L* referred to a "savings and loan" banking crisis that was transpiring at the time.) Gates followed up the showy performance by appearing on nationally viewed television programs and sitting down for interviews with reporters.

Windows 3.0 might not have buttered people's toast, but consumers found its point and click system a breeze to use. By October 1990, Microsoft had shipped more than one million units of Windows 3.0.[10] The few other computer operating systems available became all but obsolete. Just about every computer user, other than Macintosh owners, were soon using Microsoft software. Gates declared publicly that Microsoft had won the battle of the GUI.[11]

As a result of the

S & L Crisis

A savings and loan (S & L) association is a type of financial institution that provides funds for building or buying homes. They also offer other services, such as checking accounts, savings accounts, and insurance. Some are owned by the people who keep their money there, while others are owned by stockholders. The first American savings and loan opened in 1831 in Pennsylvania. During the 1980s, more than a thousand savings and loan associations went bankrupt and hundreds of others were on the verge of failing. There were many reasons why this was happening: the savings and loans were not properly controlled by the government; they had trouble competing with other financial service institutions; some of the people in charge were using the money for their own ends; and many of the customers could not pay back their loans.

In 1989, Congress passed laws to resolve the crisis and stop it from happening again, which cost taxpayers billions of dollars.

sales of Windows 3.0, Microsoft stock prices skyrocketed and Gates and his employees were becoming very wealthy. In fact, Gates was by now the richest person in the United States.

Bill Gates continued to tinker with and make improvements to Windows 3.0. As a result, Windows 3.1 and Windows 3.11 were released over the next few years.

Now that he was in his mid-thirties, Gates began to think a little more about a life outside work. The days of sleeping in the office were becoming a thing of the past. Gates bought some land overlooking Lake Washington in the nearby town of Medina, and he hired an architect to design a dream mansion. He put a lot of thought into the project, but it would take years to build.

Meanwhile, Bill and Melinda were seeing each other periodically. Although he dated other women, he always seemed to gravitate toward Melinda. The couple made plans to become engaged.

Gates wanted a special way to propose to Melinda. On March 20, 1993, the couple was in California. They boarded a chartered airplane supposedly to take them back to Seattle. Instead, Gates had the plane diverted to Omaha, Nebraska, home of a friend named Warren Buffett. Like Gates, Buffett is a billionaire, although he made his fortune in banking and investing, not computers.

Bill Gates's "dream mansion" in Medina, Washington.

When the plane landed in Omaha, Buffett met Bill and Melinda. He took them to a jewelry store he owned and opened it just for them. With the store to themselves, Bill and Melinda picked out an engagement ring.

Gates showed that he had a sense of humor when he and Melinda helped celebrate Buffett's birthday later that year. Gates made a personal movie that featured him traveling great distances looking for background information about Buffett. At each stop, he called Melinda from a pay telephone. After Gates hung up the phone, he would look inside the coin slot for loose change.

At one point in the movie, he calls Melinda and tells her that Buffett has replaced him as the richest man in America. The phone suddenly goes dead, as if Melinda had hung up on Gates upon hearing he is no longer number one. Gates stammers into the phone, "Melinda, Melinda. You still there? Hello?"[12]

"His is the ultimate revenge of the nerd."

Bill and Melinda were married on New Year's Day, 1994, on Lanai, one of the Hawaiian Islands.

Gates was the wealthiest man in the country, he was providing a service millions of people needed, and he was married to the woman he loved.

Soon afterward, a reporter said of Gates, "His is the ultimate revenge of the nerd."[13]

8

"FROM THOSE TO WHOM MUCH IS GIVEN, MUCH IS EXPECTED"

Married life changed Gates, but only to a degree at first. He still worked long hours, but he no longer put in ninety-hour work-weeks. He started a charitable group, the William H. Gates Foundation, in 1994. Most of the foundation's money was used to fund health causes.

What did not change was Gates's skill as a business promoter. In fact, many business experts say that is what made Bill Gates a multibillionaire.

On August 24, 1995, Gates introduced to the public Windows 95. Like that day in 1990 when he showed the world what Windows 3.0 could do, Gates presented Windows 95 in a partylike atmosphere. Roughly twenty-five hundred invited guests were on hand near Microsoft headquarters. That included media from all over the world. Gates even went to the extent of getting a nationally known celebrity, *The Tonight Show* host Jay Leno, to be master of ceremonies for the event.

Windows 95 was cleaner and easier to use than earlier versions of Windows. It also included software with the capacity to use CD-ROMs, faxes, and modems to connect to the Internet. Within a week after its release, Microsoft had sold a million copies of Windows 95.[1] That amounted to about $90 million worth of sales.[2]

Consumer groups and competitors were concerned that Microsoft was becoming a monopoly.

Including all these features in one software package did more than make Bill Gates wealthier. It earned him more enemies. Consumer groups and competitors were concerned that Microsoft was becoming a monopoly. That means they felt it was very difficult or even impossible for other companies to compete. In the past, software for features such as compact discs and fax machines were usually purchased separately from the operating system. Now, these extra features were bought with the Microsoft operating software that was needed to work most personal computers.

If Microsoft was indeed a monopoly, the federal government would become involved to make sure all

Bill Gates is photographed with his wife, Melinda, outside Buckingham Palace on March 2, 2005, shortly after being knighted by Queen Elizabeth for his contributions to enterprise.

software companies had a fair shake. One publication, *The Economist*, wrote in 1995 that Gates may not yet be guilty of owning a monopoly on computer software. However, it added: "That said, it would also be wise to keep an eye on the formidable Mr. Gates. Microsoft could develop its business in ways that would warrant action by the regulators. For instance, Mr. Gates may overstretch the definition of an 'operating system.'"[3]

By that fall, Gates had more money in his personal stock portfolio than many nations have in their treasury. He was worth $13.4 billion dollars.[4] Though Paul Allen was no longer involved in the day-to-day operations of Microsoft, he did sit on the company's board of directors. He offered his advice on long-term projects and other business decisions. Allen owned 9.6 percent of Microsoft, and he was worth $5.3 billion.[5]

Like a good businessman, Bill Gates knew the meaning of diversifying, or investing in more than one product. He wrote a book titled, *The Road Ahead*. In it he discussed the history of computers going back to the 1930s and his early experimenting with computers. Gates also offered a look at the future of the computer industry. Appropriately, people who bought *The Road Ahead* got a free CD-ROM with the book. Profits from the book were donated to charity.

Gates continued to display his business sense over the next several months by diversifying even more.

In the fall of 1995, he made a blockbuster purchase for his digital library business, Corbis Corporation. One of the largest collections of historic photographs and other images was the Bettmann Archive. When a producer of a documentary film or the publisher of a nonfiction books needed specific historic images, he or she would buy them from the Bettmann Archive.

By 1995 Gates had enough money to buy the entire Bettmann Archive collection for Corbis. That amounted to an amazing 16 million film and digital images.[6] Corbis Corporation was now one of the world's biggest historic image collections.

Then in 1996, Gates expanded into a completely new direction. He founded a cable television news network in association with the existing television network, National Broadcasting Company (NBC). It is called MSNBC, or Microsoft NBC, and it first went on the air on July 15, 1996. It was originally meant to be part of a new medium, "interactive TV."[7] It would consist of two services: the cable news network and an Internet information source. The founding of MSNBC was the first major attempt to compete with the original all-news cable network, CNN.

Like a **good businessman, Bill Gates knew the meaning of diversifying.**

There was further expansion in Gates's life in 1996.

Gates's wife, Melinda, gave birth to a baby girl on April 26, 1996. She was named Jennifer Katharine Gates, and she suddenly turned one of the world's most famous businesspersons into a doting father. When Jennifer was three, Gates said, "She's a little redhead with brown eyes, the happiest person I've ever met. Everything she does is just so fascinating. Just getting up in the morning . . . 'Dah-dee, can I get up now?' So I go in and pick her up. I like carrying her around a lot and she likes to be carried around."[8]

Gates also released a second edition of *The Road Ahead* in 1996. The popularity of the Internet had exploded that year. Many critics of Gates said he was late to recognize the popularity of the Internet. Gate admitted so in the preface to the second edition. He wrote: "I'm surprised by how quickly it's happening and by the way it's happening. Although I used the early Internet as a student in the 1970s, I didn't expect then that the Internet's protocols would become the standard for a network everybody would be talking about twenty years later."[9] He said in the book the Internet had gotten so popular that a panhandler he met on a Seattle street told Gates he had his own Web site.[10] Microsoft has its own Web browser, Internet Explorer, to connect personal computers to the Internet.

By 1997, Gates's mansion was finished to the point that Gates, his wife, and daughter could permanently

Bill and Melinda Gates in attendance at the groundbreaking of the University of Washington's new law school facility, William H. Gates Hall, on May 4, 2001. The Bill & Melinda Gates Foundation contributed $12 million towards the construction of the building.

move in. The sprawling estate cost an estimated $75 million to build.[11] It included a swimming pool, beach house, exercise room, dining room that can seat 120 people, and naturally, a computer room. Most functions in the main house, such as temperature controls and lights, are run by a master computer.

That year, a business magazine, *Fortune*, declared Gates the richest person in American history.[12] The value of his fortune was estimated at roughly $35 billion.[13] He had more money than any person could ever need and he started to give serious thought to what to do with his money.

For some time, critics had complained that Gates was stingy with his fortune. That was not entirely fair since he had his William H. Gates Foundation. He had also donated millions of dollars to organizations in the Seattle area for years. These included the University of Washington, the Fred Hutchinson Cancer Research Center, and various civic groups and schools. But considering that he was worth billions of dollars, to many people those donations seemed puny.

That year, a business magazine, *Fortune*, declared Gates the richest person in American history.

Gates's parents, William, Jr., and Mary, encouraged him to be more generous. Mary wrote her son a letter letting him know that his awesome wealth gave him special opportunities as well as responsibilities. She wrote: "From those to whom much is given, much is expected."[14]

In September 1997, Bill and Melinda Gates started a new charitable organization, the Gates Library Foundation. Its purpose is to bring computers and digital services to public libraries in the United States and Canada. The Gateses and Microsoft got the foundation going with a donation of $400 million.[15]

This did not silence all of his critics. They said Gates had a selfish motive, as these computers would be filled with Microsoft software. A frustrated Gates

Bill and Melinda Gates interact with some children in New Dehli, India, in December 2005. During this visit to the country, it was announced that Microsoft planned to invest $400 million in India in the upcoming years.

replied, "People are going to second-guess anything you do."[16]

At the same time, the accusations that Microsoft was a monopoly did not go away. In March 1998, Gates testified in front of a group of congresspersons in Washington, D.C. He urged the government to stay out of the computer business, stating that software engineers know better than politicians how to design software.

> **Suddenly Bill Gates, the lovable nerd who made good, was portrayed as a business bully.**

Gates released the new Windows 98 in July 1998. Many who owned Windows 95 upgraded their software. Almost all those who bought new computers in 1998 used Windows 98 software because most new computers had Windows 98 already installed.

This may have meant automatic sales for Windows, but it troubled many. Competitors and the U.S. Justice Department alike felt that this proved that Microsoft had a monopoly on PC operating systems. In October 1998, Microsoft was officially put on trial. The U.S. Justice Department along with twenty states sued Microsoft for unfairly stifling competition.

The trial made news across the world. Suddenly Bill Gates, the lovable nerd who made good, was portrayed as a business bully. A bizarre incident that year summed up his enemies' feelings. While Gates was on business in Belgium, two young men threw four cream tarts in his face. They said their goal was to ridicule powerful people who act more important than they really are. The men were tried, punished, and sentenced to pay a small fine. Gates cracked a joke about the incident, saying he wished the pastries had tasted better.

The trial dragged on into 1999. It may have distracted Gates, but it did not stop him from being productive. His second book, *Business @ the Speed of Thought*, was published that year. Gates said that it was not a technical book as much as an advice book. He said:

> *I wrote* Business @ the Speed of Thought *to help business leaders understand how they can take advantage of the incredible changes taking place. I think business will change more in the next 10 years than it has in the last 50 and businesses that seize the opportunity and use digital tools to move information inside their enterprise, as well as to reach out to customers in new ways, they'll lead in this era.*[17]

On May 23, 1999, Melinda Gates gave birth to their second child. It was a son, named Rory John Gates. That same year Gates merged the William H.

Gates Foundation and the Gates Library Foundation to create the Bill and Melinda Gates Foundation. Its purpose is to fund a wide range of causes. These include global health improvement, providing scholarships for needy students, supplying libraries with top-of-the-line equipment, and helping regional charities in the Pacific Northwest.

Gates may have been doing good things with his money, but the trial against Microsoft continued through the summer. In November 1999, U.S. District Judge Thomas Penfield Jackson declared that Microsoft was guilty of unfair business practices. According to Jackson, Microsoft had become a controlling giant. A punishment would be decided later.

Most businesses have one individual responsible for overseeing the entire company. That person's title is usually chief executive officer (CEO). However, other people head different divisions and work under the CEO. One person might be a CFO, or chief financial officer, in charge of money matters. A computer company might have a chief technology officer, or CTO. At Microsoft, Gates himself had held nearly all those positions. It had gotten to the point that he decided he was responsible for more than he wanted.

On January 13, 2000, Gates announced that he was quitting his job as Microsoft CEO. Longtime coworker Steve Ballmer would take on that position. Gates created a new role for himself, chairman and

Bill and Melinda Gates speak with Tatomkhulu-Xhosa, a tuberculosis sufferer, in Cape Town, South Africa, on July 10, 2006. The Gateses were touring the country to learn more about efforts to fight TB and HIV/AIDS in Africa.

chief software architect. In that position he could spend his time doing what he really loved: creating software. He said, "I certainly enjoyed being the CEO. However, what I really enjoy the most is working with the product groups."[18]

In mid-February, Microsoft introduced its first product without Gates as CEO. It was the upgraded Windows 2000.

In June 2000, U.S. District Judge Jackson ruled on Microsoft's "punishment." He ordered that Microsoft be split into two separate companies. One would create and sell operating systems. The other would be responsible for all remaining aspects of the business. According to Judge Jackson, his decision would enable smaller companies to compete fairly with this titan of software.

"I certainly enjoyed being the CEO. However, what I really enjoy the most is working with the product groups."

Legally, a person or company found guilty of certain crimes is permitted to file for an appeal, or a new trial. Gates and his fellow executives immediately did so. They argued that splitting Microsoft into two companies would hurt its ability to be innovative.

Filing for an appeal turned out to be the right

decision. On June 28, 2001, a federal appeals court ruled that Judge Jackson's ruling was too harsh. The appeals court stated that a different judge should hear the case. So the case was reopened and Judge Colleen Kollar-Kotelly was assigned to it.

Judge Kollar-Kotelly suggested that instead of another time-consuming trial, Microsoft and the federal government should work toward a settlement. In a settlement, lawyers for the two sides work out an agreement rather than a judge or jury doing so. On November 2, 2001, a settlement was reached between the U.S. Department of Justice and the individual suing states and Microsoft.

In the end, Microsoft came out pretty well. It would not have to split into two companies. However, it did have to make changes in its practices. For example, Microsoft would have to enable computer users to remove access to certain Windows components from their computers. Microsoft was also banned from retaliating against competitors. Microsoft was also forced to allow rival companies to plug their products into Windows operating systems.[19]

The next year, Melinda Gates gave birth to the couple's third child, a girl named Phoebe Adele. And Microsoft continued releasing new products. In addition to software and operating systems, Microsoft introduced the Xbox video-game system and a slew of personal computer games.

But as Gates approached fifty years old, he was making more news for his philanthropy and less for software. In fact, some observers put aside their concerns about Microsoft being a monopoly. To them, the good things Gates did with his money outweighed any negative effects of Microsoft's business practices. After the Bill and Melinda Gates Foundation donated $1 billion for scholarships for qualified minority students, an African-American congressperson had only praise for Gates. Texas Democratic representative Eddie Bernice Johnson proclaimed, "Instead of focusing on bringing down Bill Gates, we need to invest our resources in more Bill Gateses."[20]

The Bill and Melinda Gates Foundation donated $1 billion for scholarships for qualified minority students.

By 2004, Gates was by far the richest person in the world, worth about $46.6 billion.[21] He was also the world's largest private giver.[22] In honor of his charity, in 2004 Gates was officially given an honorary knighthood by the British government, despite the fact that he is not a British citizen.

Nowadays, when Bill Gates is in the news, he is likely to be talking about discovering vaccines rather than software. He and his wife, Melinda, are more

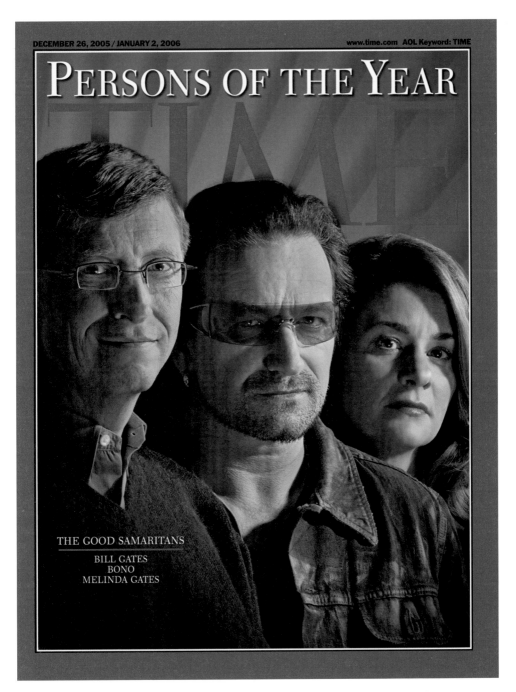

In 2005, Bill and Melinda Gates were named (along with music star, Bono) "Persons of the Year" in honor of their many humanitarian and charitable efforts.

often seen visiting slums in the world's poorest places than inside a building at Microsoft headquarters. They meet firsthand with people who will be given the medicines and vaccines they helped provide.

In 2005, they visited the poverty-stricken Asian nation of Bangladesh. As they landed at the airport, the Gateses were welcomed with huge portraits of themselves and a sign reading, "LONG LIVE BILL AND MELINDA GATES."[23]

By 2004, Gates was by far the richest person in the world. He was also the world's largest private giver.

By the end of 2005, the Bill and Melinda Gates Foundation had given hundreds of millions of dollars to develop a vaccine to cure the disease, AIDS. The foundation has been credited with saving more than seven hundred thousand lives across the world. It has provided computers and Internet access to eleven thousand libraries in North America.[24] The foundation provides about one third of the world's funding in fighting malaria, a sometimes fatal disease spread by infected mosquitoes. The natural medicine used to treat malaria is in short supply. But in April 2006, scientists funded by the Gates foundation announced they had created the ability to make an artificial version of the same medication. Hundreds of thousands of more lives now can be saved.

Gates did not lose total interest in creating new products. In May 2006, he appeared at the Electronic Entertainment Expo in Los Angeles to promote all sorts of new ideas for home entertainment. However, he really wanted to spend more time with the Bill and Melinda Gates Foundation.

On June 15, 2006, Gates announced that he is officially retiring from his software development job at Microsoft. To allow his business to adjust to the change in leadership, he will continue with his job until 2008. At that time, Steve Ballmer and chief technical officers Ray Ozzie and Craig Mundie will control the reins of Microsoft.

> **The Gateses were welcomed with huge portraits of themselves and a sign reading, "LONG LIVE BILL AND MELINDA GATES."**

However, Gates will not stay totally out of the software business. While Ballmer, Ozzie, and Mundie will be in charge of Microsoft's day-to-day activities, Gates will serve as Microsoft's chairman. He will also be an adviser on key development projects.

For example, early in 2007 he showed off to reporters and members of the electronics industry a slew of new Microsoft technological products. Some extend way beyond personal computing. One was Sync, a voice-activated technology Microsoft developed together with Ford Motor. It allows automobile drivers to perform hand-free phone dialing, receive incoming text messages through the car's audio system, and adjust digital music players using voice commands or controls on their steering wheels.

Gates also demonstrated at the time Vista OS, Microsoft's first major Windows operating system upgrade in more than five years. He further discussed Microsoft's plans to make IPTV service, or television programming received by way of high-sped Internet connections, available through Xbox 360 gaming consoles.

Gates said, "As everything is more connected, the user is in more control every year. And we want to give them more tools to do that."[25]

Gates echoed the words of his mother when he said, "Of course, with the success of Microsoft, I've also been given the gift of great wealth. I believe that with great wealth comes great responsibility—a responsibility to give back to society and to see that those resources are put

> **"I believe that with great wealth comes great responsibility—a responsibility to give back to society. . ."**

to work in the best possible way to help those most in need."[26]

When a television interviewer asked Gates if he is reluctant to give up his main duties at Microsoft, Gates answered, "I'll only be part-time doing great software. And that's been my life's work. And I'm sure I'm gonna miss that. But I get to fill it in with another thing that excites me—and challenges me."[27]

Just days later, Gates's friend and fellow multibillionaire Warren Buffett made a startling public announcement. He is going to give away 85 percent of his personal fortune of $44 billion—most of it to the Bill and Melinda Gates Foundation.[28]

CHRONOLOGY

1955   William Henry Gates III born on October 28 in Seattle, Washington.

1960   Begins public school.

1962   Inspired by visit to Seattle World's Fair.

1967   First attends private Lakeside School.

1968   First works with computers; meets Paul Allen; Lakeside Programmers Group started.

1971   Starts Traf-O-Data business with Allen.

1972   Works summer as congressional page.

1973   Works salaried job for TRW with Allen to look for computer bugs; starts college at Harvard University in fall.

1975   With Allen, sells software system for the Altair, early personal computer, to MITS in Albuquerque, New Mexico.

1976   Founds Microsoft with Allen in Albuquerque; writes "An Open Letter to Hobbyists"; business deals with General Electric and National Cash Register.

1977   Formally drops out of college.

In December 1979 and January 1980, **1979–1980**
moves Microsoft headquarters from Albuquerque,
New Mexico, to Seattle, Washington.

Makes blockbuster deal with International **1980**
Business Machines (IBM) on November 6.

IBM PC introduced to public on August 12. **1981**

Microsoft releases Multiplan spreadsheet **1982**
software.

Microsoft releases Microsoft Word. **1983**

Windows 1.0 released on November 21. **1985**

Microsoft stock goes public on March 13. **1986**

Meets future wife, Melinda French; **1987**
Windows 2.03 released in October; first
Microsoft CD-ROM released; becomes youngest
millionaire in United States history.

Apple files suit against Microsoft. **1988**

Court rules in favor of Microsoft against **1989**
Apple in March; founds Corbis Corporation.

Microsoft introduces Windows 3.0 on **1990**
May 22. Microsoft Encarta, an encylopedia
software program, is released.

Marries Melinda French on January 1 in **1994**
Hawaii; William H. Gates Foundation started.

1995 Windows 95 introduced on August 24; *The Road Ahead* is first published; buys Bettmann Archive for Corbis.

1996 Daughter Jennifer Katharine born on April 26; cable news network MSNBC first airs on July 15.

1997 Moves into unfinished mansion; named richest person in United States history; Gates Library Foundation founded in September.

1998 Windows 98 released in July; U.S. Justice Department and twenty states file charges of unfair business practices against Microsoft— trial starts in October.

1999 Second book, *Business @ the Speed of Thought* is published; son Rory John Gates born on May 23; Bill and Melinda Gates Foundation founded; Microsoft found guilty of unfair business practices.

2000 Leaves position as Microsoft CEO on January 13; Windows 2000 released in February; in June, judge orders Microsoft to be split into two companies—Microsoft appeals judge's ruling.

Federal appeals court rules in favor of **2001**
Microsoft on June 28; settlement reached in
unfair business practices case on November 2.

Daughter Phoebe Adele Gates born; Xbox **2002**
game system introduced.

Awarded honorary knighthood by British **2004**
government for charitable work.

Announces retirement from most duties at **2006**
Microsoft on June 15; billionaire Warren
Buffet announces on June 26 he will leave
most of his fortune to Bill & Melinda Gates
Foundation.

Introduces Sync, Vista OS, and plans to **2007**
make iPTV service available through
Xbox 360 gaming consoles.

CHAPTER NOTES

Chapter 1. Celebrating With a Shirley Temple and Ice Cream

1. Stephen Manes and Paul Andrews, *Gates: How Microsoft's Mogul Reinvented an Industry—and Made Himself the Richest Man in America* (New York: Doubleday, 1993), pp. 73–74.

2. James Wallace and Jim Erickson, *Hard Drive: Bill Gates and the Making of the Microsoft Empire* (New York: HarperBusiness, 1992), p. 79.

3. Ibid.

4. Manes and Andrews, p. 75.

Chapter 2. Lakeside Mothers Club to the Rescue

1. Stephen Manes and Paul Andrews, *Gates: How Microsoft's Mogul Reinvented an Industry—and Made Himself the Richest Man in America* (New York: Doubleday, 1993), p. 15.

2. Winda Benedetti, "The Future Isn't What They Thought It Would Be Back in 1962," *Seattle Post-Intelligencer*, April 18, 2002, <http://seattlepi.nwsource.com/lifestyle/66879_fairfuture.shtml> (June 8, 2006).

3. Ibid.

4. Ibid.

5. Ibid.

6. Manes and Andrews, p. 22.

7. "Remarks by Bill Gates, Co-chair, Lakeside School, September 23, 2005," Bill and Melinda Gates

Foundation Web site, n.d., <http://www.gatesfoundation.
org/MediaCenter/Speeches/Co-ChairSpeeches/
BillgSpeeches/BGSpeechLakeside-050923.htm>
(June 14, 2006).

8. James Wallace and Jim Erickson, *Hard Drive:
Bill Gates and the Making of the Microsoft Empire*
(New York: HarperBusiness, 1992), p. 21.

Chapter 3. Bugs in the Machines

1. "Remarks by Bill Gates, Co-chair, Lakeside
School, September 23, 2005," Bill and Melinda Gates
Foundation Web site, n.d., <http://www.gatesfoundation.
org/MediaCenter/Speeches/Co-ChairSpeeches/
BillgSpeeches/BGSpeechLakeside-050923.htm>
(June 14, 2006).

2. Stephen Manes and Paul Andrews, *Gates: How
Microsoft's Mogul Reinvented an Industry—and Made
Himself the Richest Man in America* (New York:
Doubleday, 1993), pp. 29–30.

3. "Remarks by Bill Gates, Co-chair, Lakeside
School, September 23, 2005," Bill and Melinda Gates
Foundation Web site.

4. Ibid.

5. Bill Gates, *The Road Ahead: Completely Revised
and Up-to-Date* (New York: Penguin Books, 1996),
p. 14.

6. James Wallace and Jim Erickson, *Hard Drive:
Bill Gates and the Making of the Microsoft Empire*
(New York: HarperBusiness, 1992), p. 45.

7. Manes and Andrews, p. 45.

8. "Bill Gates: A Profile," BBC News World
Edition, February 10, 2000, <http://news.bbc.co.uk/

2/hi/in_depth/business/2000/microsoft/633910.stm>
(June 14, 2006).

9. "Remarks by Bill Gates, Co-chair, Lakeside
School, September 23, 2005," Bill and Melinda Gates
Foundation Web site.

10. Wallace and Erickson, p. 49.

Chapter 4. "We Hope Not a Turkey"

1. "In With the New: Predictions for 2005," Ziff
Davis Marketing Zone Web site, <http://www.ziffdavis.
com/products/research/archived/zone.19.html>
(June 20, 2006); also: "On the Lighter Side: Prophetic
Quotes," *Coen Online Newsletter*, Boise State University,
May 12, 2006, <http://coen.boisestate.edu/pr/news.
asp?id=27> (June 20, 2006).

2. James Wallace and Jim Erickson, *Hard Drive:
Bill Gates and the Making of the Microsoft Empire*
(New York: HarperBusiness, 1992), p. 60.

3. Walter Isaacson, "In Search of the Real Bill
Gates," EBSCOhost, originally appeared in *Time*,
January 13, 1997.

4. Stephen Manes and Paul Andrews, *Gates: How
Microsoft's Mogul Reinvented an Industry—and Made
Himself the Richest Man in America* (New York:
Doubleday, 1993), p. 89.

5. Ibid., pp. 89–90.

6. Andrew Leonard, "Do-it-yourself giant brains!"
Salon, June 22, 2000, <http://archive.salon.com/tech/
fsp/2000/06/22/chapter_2_part_two/index4.html>
(June 23, 2006).

7. Ibid.

8. Manes and Andrews, p. 92.

Chapter 5. Long Days in the Desert

1. J. D. Reed, Todd Gold, Tom Cunneff, and Tina Kelley, "25 Legends of the past 25 years: Bill Gates," EBSCOhost, originally appeared in *People*, March 15, 1999, <http://search.ebscohost.com/> (June 16, 2006).

2. Stephen Manes and Paul Andrews, *Gates: How Microsoft's Mogul Reinvented an Industry—and Made Himself the Richest Man in America* (New York: Doubleday, 1993), p. 101.

3. James Wallace and Jim Erickson, *Hard Drive: Bill Gates and the Making of the Microsoft Empire* (New York: HarperBusiness, 1992), p. 112.

4. Bill Gates, *The Road Ahead: Completely Revised and Up-to-Date* (New York: Penguin Books, 1996), pp. 46–47.

5. Columbia University Web site, June 28, 2006, <http://www.columbia.edu/~xs23/invest.htm> (June 16, 2006).

Chapter 6. Dressing Up for IBM

1. Brent Schlender and Henry Goldblatt, "Bill Gates & Paul Allen Talk," EBSCOhost, originally appeared in *Fortune*, October 2, 1995, <http://search.ebscohost.com/> (April 11, 2006).

2. David Gelernter, "Bill Gates," in *Time 100—Builders & Titans: Great Minds of the Century*, Kelly Knauer, ed. (New York: Time Books, 1999), p. 83.

3. Schlender and Goldblatt.

Chapter 7. "It's All About the Gooey"

1. Ifilm Web site, n.d., <http://www.ifilm.com/ ifilmdetail/2423862> (July 10, 2006).

2. Kevin Maney, "Apple's '1984' Super Bowl Commercial Still Stands as Watershed Event," *USA Today* Web site, January 28, 2004, <http://www. usatoday.com/tech/columnist/kevinmaney/2004-01-28-maney_x.htm> (July 10, 2006).

3. Ibid.

4. James Wallace and Jim Erickson, *Hard Drive: Bill Gates and the Making of the Microsoft Empire* (New York: HarperBusiness, 1992), p. 301.

5. Walter Isaacson, "In Search of the Real Bill Gates," *EBSCOhost*, originally appeared in *Time*, January 13, 1997, <http://search.ebscohost.com/> (April 10, 2006).

6. Wallace and Erickson, p. 329.

7. Ibid.

8. Bill Gates, *The Road Ahead: Completely Revised and Up-to-Date* (New York: Penguin Books, 1996), pp. 257–258.

9. J. Schwartz, "Bill Gates' New Windows," EBSCOhost, originally appeared in *Newsweek*, May 21, 1990, <http://search.ebscohost.com/> (July 14, 2006).

10. Paul Andrews, *How the Web Was Won* (New York: Broadway Books, 1999), p. 50.

11. Ibid.

12. Isaacson.

13. Philip Elmer-DeWitt, "Bill Gates," EBSCOhost, originally appeared in *Time*, December 25, 1995–January 1, 1996, <http://search.ebscohost.com/> (April 11, 2006).

Chapter 8. "From Those to Whom Much Is Given, Much Is Expected"

1. James Kim, "Windows 95: 1 Million Copies Sold So Far," *USA Today* Web site, originally ran August 30, 1995, <http://search.ebscohost.com/> (July 17, 2006).

2. Ibid.

3. "How Dangerous Is Microsoft?" EBSCOhost, originally appeared in *The Economist*, July 8, 1995, <http://search.ebscohost.com/> (July 17, 2006).

4. Brent Schlender and Henry Goldblatt, "Bill Gates & Paul Allen Talk," EBSCOhost, originally appeared in *Fortune*, October 2, 1995, <http://search. ebscohost.com/> (April 11, 2006).

5. Ibid.

6. "Gates' Curbis [sic] Corp. Purchase Swells Its Historical Image Archive," EBSCOhost, originally appeared in *CD-ROM Professional*, February 1996, <http://search.ebscohost.com/> (July 17, 2006).

7. Laurent Belsie, "NBC, Microsoft Launch Interactive News Service," EBSCOhost, originally appeared in *The Christian Science Monitor*, July 15, 1996, <http://search.ebscohost.com/> (July 17, 2006).

8. Steven Levy, "Behind the Gates Myth," EBSCOhost, originally appeared in *Newsweek*, August 30, 1999, <http://search.ebscohost.com/> (April 10, 2006).

9. Bill Gates, *The Road Ahead: Completely Revised*

and Up-to-Date (New York: Penguin Books, 1996), p. ix.

10. Ibid., p. xii.

11. Robert Slater, *Microsoft Rebooted: How Bill Gates and Steve Ballmer Reinvented Their Company* (New York: Penguin Group, 2004), p. 120.

12. Randall E. Stross, "Bill Gates: Richest American Ever," EBSCOhost, originally appeared in *Fortune*, August 4, 1997, <http://search.ebscohost.com/> (April 10, 2006).

13. Ibid.

14. Amanda Ripley, "From Riches to Rags," *Time*, December 26, 2005, p. 83.

15. "Gates, Microsoft Donate $400 Million to Libraries," EBSCOhost, originally appeared in *Computers in Libraries*, September 1997, <http://search.ebscohost.com/> (June 16, 2006).

16. Levy.

17. "Bill Gates Remarks on *Business @ the Speed of Thought*," Bill Gates Web site, March 31, 1999, <http://www.microsoft.com/billgates/speedofthought/looking/qanda.aspx> (July 18, 2006).

18. Bob Trott and Michael Lattig, "Bill Gates Steps Aside as Microsoft's CEO," EBSCOhost, originally appeared in *InfoWorld*, January 17, 2000, <http://search.ebscohost.com/> (April 11, 2006).

19. Slater, p. 46.

20. Ronald Roach, "Gates Talks Tech With Supportive Black Caucus," EBSCOhost, originally appeared in *Black Issues in Higher Education*, July 6, 2000, <http://search.ebscohost.com/> (April 10, 2006).

21. "Gates Thinks Big, Gives Big," CNN Web site, April 20, 2004, <http://www.cnn.com/2004/WORLD/americas/04/16/gates/index.html> (April 11, 2006).

22. Ibid.

23. Geoffrey Cowley, "Keeping Up With the Gateses," *Newsweek*, December 19, 2005, p. 50.

24. Ripley, p. 77.

25. Jon Swartz, "Gates Previews New Wave of Products to Keep User in Control," *USA Today*, January 8, 2007, p. 6A.

26. Benjamin Romano, "Gates' Next Full-time Job: Trying to Save the World," *The Seattle Times* Web site, June 16, 2006, <http://archives.seattletimes.nwsource.com/cgi-bin/texis.cgi/web/vortex/display?slug=microsoft16&date=20060616&query=%22gates%27+next+full-time+job%22> (June 16, 2006).

27. Campbell Brown interview with Bill Gates, *The Today Show*, NBC television network, originally broadcast July 18, 2006, <http://www.msnbc.com/id/13910240>.

28. Carol J. Loomis, "Warren Buffet Gives Away His Fortune," *Fortune*, CNNMoney.com Web site, June 25, 2006, <http://money.cnn.com/2006/06/25/magazines/fortune/charity1.fortune/index.htm> (July 20, 2006).

FURTHER READING

Boyd, Aaron. *Smart Money: The Story of Bill Gates.* Greensboro, N.C.: Morgan Reynolds, 2004.

Desouza, Lar, and Mattie J. T. Stepanek. *Boys Who Rocked the World: From King Tut to Tiger Woods.* Hillsboro, Oreg.: Beyond Words Publishing, 2001.

French, Laura. *Internet Pioneers: The Cyber Elite.* Berkeley Heights, N.J.: Enslow Publishers, 2001.

Lee, Lauren. *Bill Gates.* Milwaukee: World Almanac Library, 2002.

Lesinski, Jeanne. *Bill Gates.* Minneapolis, Minn.: Lerner Publications Company, 2000.

Romanek, Trudee. *The Technology Book for Girls.* Toronto, Canada: Kids Can Press, 2001.

Sherman, Joseph. *Bill Gates: Computer King.* Brookfield, Conn.: Millbrook Press, 2000.

Webster, Christine. *Washington* ("From Sea to Shining Sea" series). New York: Children's Press, 2003.

INTERNET ADDRESSES

The official site of Microsoft
http://www.microsoft.com

The Bill and Melinda Gates Foundation
http://www.gatesfoundation.org/default.htm

The Computer History Museum in Mountain View, California
http://www.computerhistory.org/

INDEX